# CROQUET

## ITS HISTORY, STRATEGY, RULES, AND RECORDS

# CROQUET

## ITS HISTORY, STRATEGY, RULES, AND RECORDS

JAMES CHARLTON and WILLIAM THOMPSON
with ROGER, KATHERINE, and ANDREW ADLER

THE STEPHEN GREENE PRESS

Lexington, Massachusetts

THE STEPHEN GREENE PRESS, INC.

Published by the Penguin Group
Viking Penguin Inc., 40 West 23rd Street, New York, New York 10010, U.S.A.
Penguin Books Ltd, 27 Wrights Lane, London W8 5TZ, England
Penguin Books Australia Ltd, Ringwood, Victoria, Australia
Penguin Books Canada Ltd, 2801 John Street, Markham, Ontario, Canada L3R 1B4
Penguin Books (N.Z.) Ltd, 182-190 Wairau Road, Auckland 10, New Zealand

Penguin Books Ltd, Registered Offices: Harmondsworth, Middlesex, England

First published in 1977 by Turtle Press in association with Charles Scribner's Sons
This revised edition published in 1988 by The Stephen Greene Press, Inc.
Published simultaneously in Canada
Distributed by Viking Penguin Inc.

Line drawings by Katherine Adler, unless otherwise indicated
Photographs by Roger Adler, unless otherwise indicated

The text of Chapter XVIII is reprinted with permission. Copyright 1985 Jack R.
Osborn and the United States Croquet Association.

CIP data available

Printed in the United States of America
by The Alpine Press, Inc.

Set in Century Schoolbook
Designed by Andrew Bromberg

*We would like to thank the following:*

United States Croquet Association; American Croquet Association; Tom Begner; Rickie Harvey; Spencer Gale; Dr. Xandra Kayden; Archie Burchfield; Alfred Heath; G. Nigel Aspinall; Ted Prentis; H. B. Swope, Jr.; S. Joseph Tankoos; Margaret Hope; John Jaques; New York Croquet Club; Mary Alma Yousey; Mrs. Moss Hart; Library of Congress; New York Public Library; Mrs. W. Dickenson; Russ and Carol Titelman; Elva Berger; and a particular thanks to Jack Osborn.

# Contents

# CROQUET

BOSTON.
PUBLISHED BY G. D. RUSSELL & COMPANY 126 TREMONT, OPP. PARK ST.

# FOREWORD

The croquet game most of us remember has grown and changed for the better over the years until it has evolved into an even more stimulating and competitive form combining the physical and mental challenge of golf, billiards, chess and war.

Many people adept at more strenuous sports have taken up croquet as a second or third activity. Both youthful and middle-aged players have developed a keen interest in the game, and it is the primary outdoor recreation for many.

Until 1977, when the first edition of this book was published and the United Croquet Association was launched, the game's greatest weakness in America had been the lack of reliable, non-conflicting information regarding where it should be played, and by what rules. Now, updated and expanded in the following pages, these answers and much more about this great sport are again available.

From its original publication, this long needed book filled a huge vacuum in the literature on croquet in America and marked a pivotal point in the resurgence of interest in the game. Along with the many fascinating, frustrating and amusing aspects of croquet, you will also learn herein of how there is even a more challenging opportunity for our current backyard players to move up the skill scale and discover the truly interesting nuances of the American game, by adopting the techniques and rules advanced by the United States Croquet Association.

To the leaders and members of the over 300 clubs that joined the USCA since its inception, we owe a huge debt of gratitude for helping to being order out of the chaos of seventy-five years of inattentiveness to the sport in America. While they are far too many to mention in this foreword, you will be introduced to some in the U.S. Hall of Fame section in this book. Others who deserve credit for the growing interest and success that croquet is enjoying will know who they are and will surely be recognized as the Hall of Fame expands over the exciting years ahead.

Until non-Americans gain entry to our Hall, however, we would be remiss not to express our appreciation to such international greats as world champions John W. Solomon and G. Nigel Aspinall, as well as Ian Gillespie, Ron Sloane and Professor Bernard Neal—without whose hands-across-the-sea generosity and inspiration modern American croquet simply would not be.

To those families, individuals and/or clubs currently playing the 9-wicket/2-stake Double Diamond game, we urge you to try the more sophisticated 6-wicket version and become better prepared to compete with others in the dramatically growing list of U.S. Croquet Association clubs.

Similarly, to those beginners interested in forming a croquet club in your area, we extend an invitation to apply for membership in the United States Croquet Association.

Jack R. Osborn
President, USCA

# CROQUET

ITS HISTORY, STRATEGY, RULES,
AND RECORDS

# DENNIS THE MENACE

"IT'S CALLED CROQUET. IT'S SOMETHING LIKE GOLF ONLY IT'S **FUN**."

# I
# *In the Swing*

*"It's played by a lot of very intelligent people from varied back-grounds, and you don't find them wasting their time on trivial nonsense."*
—G. Nigel Aspinall
International Croquet Star
(*M Magazine*, July, 1984)

*"The most challenging sport you can play."*
—Dr. Douglas Payne
Croquet Zealot

*"Probably the most liberated sport that I know of."*
—Debbie Prentis
Croquet Champion
(*NBC Nightly News*, April 25, 1987)

These people have never been more serious. Croquet is not a pastime to them; it's a passion. They are among the thousands who have fallen under the spell of croquet and are now hooked for life.

Jane Pauley of "Today" calls croquet, "The hot backyard game of the eighties," and the popularity of the sport is indeed sky-rocketing. Stores cannot keep enough croquet sets in stock—500,000 were sold just last year. Even the venerable mallet manufacturer Jaques and Sons has been caught short, and this is nothing to sneeze at—one of their sets could set you back $1,000! Arizona croquetphile Dr. Gerald Bassford, who hand-fashions top-of-the-line mallets, is hopelessly swamped with orders.

The advertising and news media are picking up on mallet mania. Countless articles have recently appeared in magazines and newspapers, and stories of wicket ways brighten the airways. Glamorous people playing croquet are also now enhancing the sale of products—from gin to cosmetics.

Many of the Beautiful People are finding croquet's attraction addictive. Actor Louis Jourdan is in the USCA Hall of Fame, and

> *"Do I drink the wine and then take my best shot, or do I take my shot and then drink?" The slight, suave gentleman in the crisp slacks, starched shirt and soft leather walking shoes stands on the impeccable bowling green, his thin arm cocked in the idle swing of a croquet mallet, and ponders this age-old rock 'n roll question. Probation before libation? Refreshment before achievement? "I think," shouts quick-witted Patti Austin from the veranda, "that you should party and then party!"*
>
> *And so commences another thoroughly civilized summer afternoon in the life of Steve Winwood, rock's gentle aristocrat, as he sips chablis and takes a turn around the lawn wickets with equally refined noted arranger Arif Mardin. They and the rest of the guests (which include actors Griffin Dunne and Ellen Barkin) have been called together to celebrate the forty-first birthday of producer Russ Titelman and the start of Steve's fourth solo album.*
> —Timothy White, "Steve Winwood's Merging Traffic," *Musician Magazine*, July 1986.

popular singer Anne Murray is president of a mallet club. Larry Hagman, Richard Chamberlain, Cliff Robertson, George Plimpton and Judge William Rehnquist are just a few whose names are linked to mallets and wickets.

Well-known record producer Russ Titelman and his wife, Carol, set up a croquet course soon after moving to Connecticut. On Russ's birthday, croquet was offered to the guests, some of the most prominent music and entertainment figures. Most hadn't played since childhood, but once they got going, the enthusiasm mounted. The following year, as people arrived at the party, most greeted their hosts with, "Where's the croquet game?"

Carol enthusiastically states, "Croquet is a great game for a party. It provides an interesting context for people who don't know each other very well to mix and socialize." Croquet has become a Titelman tradition.

Another croquet tradition began in 1985 in Princeton, New Jersey. H. Gross & Co., posh "outfitters" to the community, wanted to do something that would bring town and gown together. Croquet seemed just the thing. Invitations were sent to Princeton University students, faculty and administrators, as well as various local leaders (including Governor Brendan Byrne). H. Gross considered their first "Invitational" such a success that they repeat

**The Beauty of Croquet—Revlon style.**

it annually.

The United States Croquet Association, now located at plush headquarters in Palm Beach, Florida, is greatly responsible for the flowering of the sport. From an idea planted at Westhampton, Long Island, in 1960, the USCA has blossomed throughout the fifty states and new clubs join every week.

The USCA distributes rules, keeps tabs on rankings, issues instructional videotapes, and promotes their sport with the slogan, "Croquet is OK!" Their school not only teaches players, but certifies new instructors and referees.

Jack R. Osborn, president of the USCA, is the self-proclaimed "Johnny Appleseed of Croquet." Sowing the seeds of croquet is so important to this one-time ad man that a rival once exclaimed, "When Jack goes, we'll have to bury him at center court with a stake through his heart to keep him from preaching croquet to the heathens" (*New York Times Sunday Magazine,* September 14, 1980).

Jack describes his obsession: "The game combines physical eye-hand coordination with tactical strategy, almost warfare-like planning. That's what attracts these very bright people. Let's face it, the business world is war. Croquet is a perfect extension of that" (*New York Times Sunday Magazine Part 2,* June 8, 1986).

3

**Teddy Prentis: a man whose time has come.**

When speaking of croquet, its adherents often wax philosophical. Teddy Prentis, winner of seven USCA titles, reasons, "If you have to cheat at croquet, you must really have problems with the rest of your life" (*M Magazine,* July 1984).

Son of USCA co-founder Edmund "Ned" Prentis III, Teddy became croquet's first full-time professional. In 1980, he and his wife, Debbie, were summoned to the Palm Beach Polo & Country Club to spread the word. The Teddy Prentis name now carries enough weight to endorse a Rolex watch.

Aside from the ad campaign, Rolex has underwritten a "Classic Pro/Celebrity Tournament" in New York's Central Park. The Croquet Foundation and the Park Conservancy split the proceeds in what promises to be an annual event. Celebrities from the croquet world, Broadway and Hollywood mingle, and the champagne flows freely.

**The Rolex Pro/Celebrity Tournament**

**Right:** Roland Puton (President and C.E.O. Rolex Watch, U.S.A.)— croquet personified.

**Left:** Anita Gillette and Gene Rayburn exchange pleasantries.

**Below:** Gene Rayburn and David Groh look on as two pros show them how it's done.

*photos by Bill Hickey*

*courtesy of Rolex Watch, USA*

Parties and croquet make an old partnership. In fact, formal socializing is a second phase of the sport. Duncan Syme, a wily Vermont inventor, has even developed a croquet wicket that holds a drink!

Privileged Palm Beachers look forward every year to the "Croquet Invitational Ball"—a highlight of the season. Reminders of the day's athletic endeavors can be seen in the white "tennies" (sneakers) sported by the tuxedo-clad gentlemen, and gaudy cummerbunds striped in black, blue, red and yellow—the four croquet colors.

Eight miles south of Asbury Park, New Jersey lies the beautiful Green Gables Croquet Club. Started in the 1950s, it is the oldest ongoing club in the United States. This lovely setting is home to croquet enthusiasts Dr. Douglas Payne and his wife, Betty. "Who in the hell plays croquet?" was the good doctor's reaction when Betty first suggested they take it up; but now he cheerfully admits he "eats, drinks and sleeps" the sport.

When asked if croquet, with its Champagne Set reputation, was a sport reserved only for the rich, Dr. Payne replied. "It costs a lot to buy equipment and maintain a lawn properly, but if a few people get together it can be done for not too much money." Jack Osborn concurs, "You don't have to be rich and from Palm Beach to play" (*Los Angeles Times,* September 30, 1986).

Archie Burchfield: "Little did I realize when I started playing croquet in a town of six hundred out behind the little Christian church that a croquet game would get me to Palm Beach." ("Lipsyte on Sports," NBC Nightly News, April 25, 1987)

*courtesy of Archie Burchfield*

Tell that to Archie Burchfield, a tobacco farmer from Stamping Ground, Kentucky, probably the most colorful character among the world's top croquet players. "It's an expensive hobby with no return." Burchfield's eyes twinkled as he grumbled to Robert Lipsyte of NBC News. "I mean I've got one hundred and twenty-two trophies at home. Those hundred and twenty-two trophies cost me thirty thousand dollars and they're not worth fifteen cents!"

In Kentucky, croquet is so popular that it is not considered a rich man's game. State-wide championship tournaments have been played for the past forty years, on clay courts, using a nine-wicket layout. The mallets are short-handled (only eighteen inches) and the smooth balls are slightly smaller than "regulation."

In 1977, Archie read an article about the USCA's first croquet championship. Intrigued, he decided to go to Palm Beach to investigate. Upon arrival, Archie and his partner were skeptically admitted into the club, but were denied food because they weren't wearing "whites."

No one ignored the tobacco farmer once they saw him play. In an exhibition, he and his partner whipped two of the world's best players. Burchfield and his son Mark, a novice, then ousted Jack Osborn and four-time champ Archie Peck in the National Doubles Championship.

"Why, we probably have one of the toughest groups right here in Kentucky," says Burchfield. "A Kentucky game is almost like war. They'll have no mercy on you." Bluegrass warriors hone their skills on the clay surfaces, where a ball travels twice as fast the Kentucky way. Archie also loves the USCA's six-wicket, grass game and calls it "the best game of croquet in the world."

Archie Burchfield foresees the development of televised croquet. All that's needed are "good commentators and prize money," he laughs, "'cause after all, who would watch golf if there wasn't one hundred thousand dollars riding on whether or not that little ball fell in the hole!"

### Go West, Young Mallet!

In 1986, The USCA broke with tradition by moving the site of the Nationals from New York to Santa Rosa, California. Brice Jones, a Sonoma vintner, lent his lush, $200,000 croquet courts for that first tournament. He also hosted a western barbecue reception, where the usual "ties and tennies" were discarded for cowpoke clothes, and the guests danced to a hoe-down band. Even the new champion was Western: Reid Fleming of Vancouver, British Columbia.

*photo by Hans Peterson*

*courtesy of Croquet Magazine*

**The Pride of Vancouver— Champion Reid Fleming**

The pampered greens of Mr. Jones now play host annually to the World Singles Championship. Called "the ultimate in croquet tournaments," it brings together the top thirty-six players from around the globe and benefits those affected by Down's syndrome.

In 1987 Stan Patmor, a founder of the Arizona Croquet Club, became the president of the newly formed American Croquet Association. The ACA promotes all forms of croquet, but particularly the American and International styles, and teaches the rules of both to its members. In the words of Vice-President Xandra Kayden, "The two games are different versions of the same sport—similar to downhill and cross-country skiing." The American Croquet Association also has a demanding clinic for referees, complete with qualifying exams.

Dr. Kayden is the founder of the New England Collegiate Croquet Association (NECCA), the mother of collegiate croquet. She once told the *New York Times* that "the Golden Age of Croquet would be at hand when Harvard plays Yale," prompting a challenge to Harvard from the Yalies. This germinated an organization that is now a growing part of the ACA. Collegiate croquet is organized by region, and includes some twenty schools. One of them, Smith College, recently installed the first competitive collegiate croquet course.

Young people represent the future of croquet, and Dr. Kayden feels that college kids "make it legitimate." She finds it exciting that she "can pair an eighty-seven-year-old man with a twenty-four-year-old and there will be an equality in the caliber of play."

Her colleague, Richard Young, agrees. Having lost a leg in World War II, he had imagined sedentary older years. Instead, taking up croquet gave him "a new lease on life." Professor Young is the founder of Smith's croquet team.

A now-legendary college croquet tournament had its start in 1983 at Annapolis, Maryland. The powerful Naval Academy received a challenge from its small but feisty neighbor, St. John's College—"three games of croquet. . . ." The winner was to have its name engraved on an ornate "Annapolis Cup."

That year and the next, St. John's took the trophy. In 1985 the Navy got its revenge, and a true croquet rivalry was assured. Johnnies are convinced that their classical academic training stands them in good stead for the mental rigors of the greensward,

*photo by Keith Harvey*

**Middies: "Well struck!" Johnnies: "Cut their budget!"**

and the Middies are, of course, filled with the necessary "warlike" attitude.

To the strains of Vivaldi and popping champagne corks, the two schools duke it out on the croquet court. Chants fill the air: "Naval Academy, school of war, school that's based on sin. St. John's College, school of knowledge, we are going to win." "We don't speak Latin, we don't know Greek, our poems don't rhyme, and we like to drive ships."

Great Britain, Australia, New Zealand, Canada and the United States are the countries where croquet is most popular, but it may soon set the world on fire. Croquet courts already dot the landscape of China, and a croquet variation called "gate ball *(gatesu-boru)*" is enjoyed by millions of Japanese. Even Russian cosmonauts are urged to unwind by indulging in wicket-ness. Bizarre croquet offshoots have appeared, including "Desert Croquet." Played in Nevada's Black Rock Desert, trucks with oversized tires smash six-foot balls through giant hoops!

One form which will doubtless catch on is "Guerilla Croquet," invented by collegiate champion Hans Peterson with his partners at *Croquet Magazine,* Bob Alman and Michael Orgill. It combines the official rules and strategy of the pro-quality sport with the less expensive equipment and rough terrain of the backyard game.

All sports have a mystique for those who love them. The beauty of croquet is you don't have to stand on the sidelines and watch—you can get involved first-hand. In the view of Jack Osborn, "Why be ranked four hundred thousandth in golf or one millionth in tennis if you can be in the top twenty of the croquet rankings?" (*New York Times Sunday Magazine,* September 14, 1980). Adds Westhampton's Alfred Heath, "The most important aspect of today's croquet is the improvement that's going on with players who started just a few years back."

No one says it will be easy, but with knowledge and dedication, you too could become part of croquet history.

*photo by Michael Orgill*

*courtesy of Croquet Magazine*

**"The Croquet Guerrilla"—A glimpse of the future?**

*The ingenuity of man has never conceived anything better calculated to bring out all the evil passions of humanity than the so-called game of croquet... Our forefathers early recognized the insidious wickedness of the game and rooted it out.*
—*Living Age,* circa 1898

*Rutherford B. Hayes also liked to play croquet on the White House lawn; but even there the Democrats would not let him alone. They charged he had squandered six dollars of taxpayers money for a set of fancy boxwood croquet balls.*
—*The American Past*
Roger Butterfield, 1957

# II
# Croquet:
# Lore and Legend

The origin of croquet, like that of many other sports, is obscure. Although the game has been played in roughly its present form for about one hundred years, its antecedents extend back many centuries. As long ago as the fourteenth century, peasants in Brittany and Southern France amused themselves playing a game called *Paille Maille,* in which crude mallets were used to knock balls through hoops made of bent willow branches. This ancestral version of croquet persisted, and by the seventeenth century, *Pele Mele,* as it was called in England, had become popular with Charles II and his court. Diarist Samuel Pepys, in his entry of April 2, 1661, wrote that "I went into St. James Parke, where I saw the Duke of Yorke playing at Pesle Mesle—the first time that I ever saw that sport." Pall Mall, as the game came finally to be called, was played with a curved club, a wooden ball, and two hoops. The court was often made of powdered cockleshells, and the hoops were decorated with flowers. The game lost favor in the 18th and 19th centuries, and little was heard of it until the 1850's.

In 1852 or 1853, croquet was introduced into England from Ireland, where a game called *crooky,* which used implements similar to the modern ones, had been played in Portarlington, Queen's County, Kilkee, in County Clare, and Kingstown, near Dublin, since the 1830's. No one knows how the game reached Ireland, although it has been suggested that it was introduced by French nuns or possibly by French refugees. According to the Oxford English Dictionary, the word "croquet" is a form of the word *croche,* an old North French word used to mean 'shepherd's crook'. The word is found in more modern French dialects, where it is used to mean 'hockey stock'. Although most agree that croquet's origin is French, it has been proposed by A.G. Ross that the game was actually born in Ireland. He claims that "croquet" came from the Irish word *cluiche,* which means 'play', and is pronounced roughly

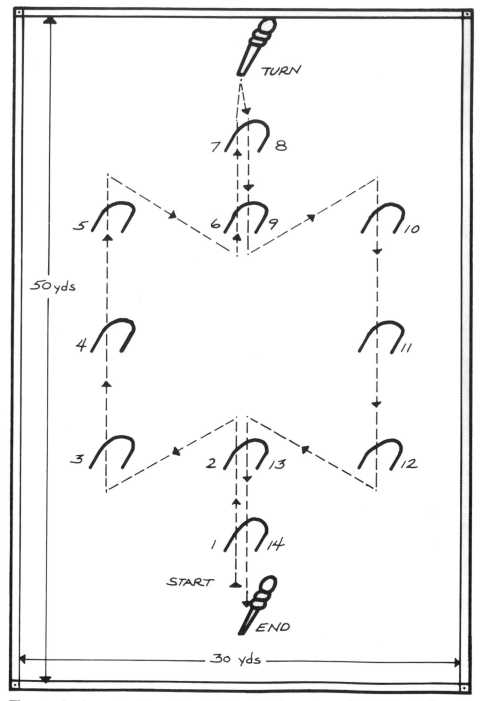

The standard court setting of the 1860's. This layout provided little challenge for the serious player.

like 'crooky'. According to Ross, the phrase "to take croquet" might be a translation of the Irish *gabail do cluiche,* which means, literally, to take to playing, or to begin to play.

Wherever its origins lie, croquet was introduced into England from Ireland in the early 1850's by one Mr. Spratt, who had been given a set of croquet implements by a Miss McNaughten around 1840. Miss McNaughten informed Mr. Spratt that the game had been introduced into Ireland but that she had seen it in its primitive state in either Southern France or Italy. The crude and rustic game observed by Miss McNaughten was played with hoops made of willow rods. The villagers constructed the mallets by boring a hole in a hard, knotty piece of wood and inserting a broomstick for the handle. Mr. Spratt kept the croquet equipment for several years before selling it to Mr. Jaques, an enterprising young man, whose family is the foremost manufacturer of croquet equipment today. It was Mr. Jaques who brought the game to notice. Incidentally, the unfortunate Miss McNaughten perished in a fire soon after giving the equipment to Mr. Spratt.

By 1865, croquet had achieved wide acceptance and had spread throughout England and its colonies. One gentleman of the time, noting in a letter to a friend that the game was introduced into India "during the hot weather of 1864 at Simla," observed that "the Viceroy played with an entire mallet of ivory—as became his position." During these early days of popularity in England, croquet was primarily an after-dinner recreation. It was played with ten large hoops, two pegs, and odd-sized mallets, on a lawn that measured 50 by 30 yards. The game was played as a sequence game, which meant that the turns *and* the balls were played sequentially according to the color of the ball. It is usually still played this way in the United States, though in Great Britain, in singles, while the turns alternate, the balls may be played in any order.

Croquet's great popularity in England continued through the 1860's and into the 1870's. In 1861, *Routledge's Handbook of Croquet* appeared. This book, probably the sport's first rule book, still basically governs the game. Another important and influential publication of the time was *Croquet: A Treatise and Commentary,* by Captain Mayne Reid, a hero of the Mexican War and the author of several books for boys. Captain Reid, whose book appeared in England in 1863 and in New York in 1869, saw croquet as a healthy, and presumably safer, substitute for war, and warned his readers of

**Members of the family of British Prime Minister Gladstone
playing croquet at Fasque, Kincardineshire in the 1860's.**

the dangers of encountering women on the croquet court.

The 1860's also saw the appearance of the game's first recorded
champions. In 1867 Walter Jones-Whitmore won a tournament at
Evesham and became, according to some, croquet's first champion.
Jones-Whitmore was also the first to attempt to devise a system of
strategy and tactics, which he published in a book called *Croquet
Tactics* in 1868. One year after Jones-Whitmore's victory at
Evesham, Walter Peel, one of the major figures in the history of
croquet, became the game's first true champion, and by 1869, the
All-England Croquet Club was founded at Wimbledon. When Peel
won his championship, the hoops were six inches wide, five inches
wide for the final two rounds. In the game's early days the hoops
had been as wide as eight inches, but they were gradually reduced in
size to four inches by 1872. Early in the 1870's lawn tennis was
introduced in England, and, for a while, the controversy over which
was the best game, tennis or croquet, became quite intense. Soon,
however, lawn tennis eclipsed croquet in popularity, and English
croquet entered a period of decline that lasted through the 1880's.

Croquet was introduced to the United States in the early 1870's.
The sport was first taken up by high society in the New York area,

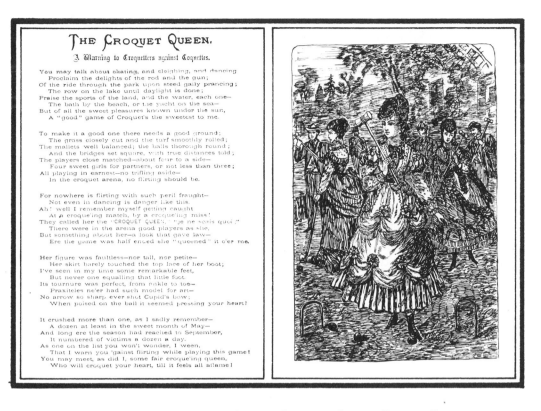

but it soon achieved general popularity throughout the country. Lawn tennis was introduced here at about the same time, but from the 1870's through the 1890's, croquet enthusiasts far outnumbered the tennis players. A croquet set was mandatory equipment for every estate, and civic leaders provided sets for public parks, which previously had not had facilities for any sport played on grass. Croquet was quite popular with women and was one of the first games played in the United States by both sexes. To this day, it is the only sport in which men and women compete with a similar handicap. Women players are more prominent today in Australia than in any other country. In 1882, the National Croquet Association was formed to help supervise the game. The association was active into the 1890's when lawn tennis suddenly surged in popularity, and croquet enthusiasm began to wane. The ebb in croquet's popularity was due, in part, to the game's surprisingly unsavory reputation. It had become associated with gambling, drinking, and philandering to such an extent that it was banned in Boston by one Reverend Skinner, and several articles of the time called upon both clergy and laity to suppress "the immoral practice of croquet."

It wasn't until the mid-1890's that interest in croquet began to revive in England, and several years later the sport's popularity began to return in the United States. Although croquet was played in a few places, tournaments had all but disappeared. The game was still played as a sequence game, with hoops whose dimensions had been reduced from four inches to three and one quarter inches in 1871. One year later, the Hale setting of six hoops and two pegs was introduced, and this setting continued in use for the next fifty years, although the hoop dimensions were again enlarged. The croquet renaissance began in 1896 when Walter Peel and Captain Drummond founded the United All-England Croquet Association at Roehampton, England. This organization, with typical British understatement, is called the Croquet Association and is still the ruling body of British and Commonwealth croquet. The final rounds of the All-England Handicap, one of croquet's most important championships, are played annually at Roehampton. Croquet's resurgence was aided by the arrival of Cyril Corbally, who, along with other great Irish players such as Duff Matthews and Leslie O'Callaghan, introduced new skills and tactics to the game. Croquet's popularity continued undiminished until the outbreak of World War I.

An ocean away, croquet's revival began in the United States. In 1899, a small group of players from the United States met in Norwich, Connecticut to revise the old Routledge Rules and revitalize the game. The new rules provided for standardized court size, reduced hoop dimensions, and the use of only four balls instead of the cumbersome eight. Two balls were used by each player, or two per team for doubles.

Croquet's popularity in the United States has been increasing since the end of World War I. In the 1930's the WPA and the National Recreation Association added croquet sets to their inventory of standard playground equipment. The sport also became a status favorite of literary and entertainment people in the '30's and '40's. East Coast players, such as George S. Kaufman, Alexander Woollcott, and Dorothy Parker, developed a fierce and unsportsman-like rivalry with West Coast players such as Harpo Marx, Darryl Zanuck, and George Sanders.

In 1922, the Willis setting of six hoops and one peg was introduced in England. This layout is still the one most used today.

Harpo Marx and George S. Kaufman at their favorite pastime.

During the mid-20's, the first test matches for the MacRobertson Shield, croquet's international trophy, were held when Australia sent a team to England. This trophy is still awarded in a competition that takes place every four years.

*He has the true croquet spirit. He trusts no one but himself; never concedes—no matter how far behind he may be—and hates his opponents with an all-enduring hate.*

—Moss Hart on Darryl Zanuck

# III
# Croquet Comes Back
# to the U.S.A.

After the First World War, American croquet, like tennis, had become a fashionable pastime or, worse yet, a game to be played occasionally with the children in the back yard.

Then in the '20's croquet became popular again, mainly through the efforts—and competition—of two men; Alexander Woollcott—author, columnist and critic—and Herbert Bayard Swope, publisher of the *New York World*, Woollcott's friend, enemy and sometime employer. Woollcott had taken his croquet mallet with him when he went away to Hamilton college and had been playing for years before his arrival in New York. Swope brought the game and equipment back from England, and together he and Woollcott helped to introduce nine-wicket, two stake, no boundaries croquet to the New York theatre and literary crowd. Woollcott was a founding member of that legendary literary set, the Algonquin Roundtable, and was probably the most experienced, and certainly fiercest, competitor among those who played. Competition was eagerly provided by Moss Hart, George Kaufman, Neysa McNein, Franklin P. Adams, Charles MacArthur, and others. Kaufman, because he was slender and had a frenzied manner of gripping the mallet, was referred to by Woollcott as "a morning glory climbing a pole." Kaufman was also the target of another barb when Richard Rodgers allowed "that Kaufman was very good in the theatre but very bad on the croquet field." Kaufman was certainly never short of the appropriate quip himself, and once, when Heywoud Broun arrived for play decked out in a grass length coat that may have cost the lives of every raccoon in New York State, Kaufman cautioned him "not to bend over in Central Park."

One of the most avid players in the group was Harpo Marx, who later helped to popularize the sport on the West Coast. Harpo was so serious a player he had a spare bedroom converted into a storeroom for his croquet equipment. It was even air conditioned to keep the

21

temperature constant and protect his purchases. Not stopping there, he talked a neighbor into letting him convert a flat-roofed garage into a practice croquet field. All told, Harpo estimated that the group spent $50,000 on equipment, a sizable sum considering the period and the fact that a comparatively small initial investment is usually all that's needed. As Kaufman recalled, "the only true winner of the game was the firm of Abercrombie and Fitch, which supplied English mallets, balls and wickets at prices just this side of keeping a string of polo ponies."

Harpo once interrupted a meeting that was going on between Alexander Woollcott and Eleanor Roosevelt by banging practice shots up and down the hallway outside Alex's apartment. Whether it was because of this or not, Woollcott eventually deserted New York for a retreat on Neshobe Island, located in the middle of Lake Bomoseen, Vermont, where he continued his writing and, of course, croquet playing. Weekend visitors were captive players for Woollcott, since he refused to allow them to return to the mainland until he had wrung a victory from them on the croquet court. As one guest put it, Woollcott "was impossible in victory, irascible in defeat." In one memorable match Harpo Marx needed only to hit, or roquet, Woollcott's ball to cinch the match, but there was a maple tree between the two balls. Harpo dragged out an old auto tire, sawed it in half, and put it around the tree, and came out the other side smacking Woollcott's ball. Furious, Alex stamped off, referring to Harpo as a "fawn's behind." Like the tale of Babe Ruth calling his home run, this story has also gotten a bit hazy with time. Another version has Harpo, confronted with the same situation, paying Woollcott's gardener $100 to dig a trench around the tree. In either case, the shot resulted in a perfect roquet.

Herbert Bayard Swope Sr., publisher of the *New York World*, was an aggressive competitor in everything he undertook, not the least of which was croquet. On his estate at Sands Point, Long Island, he built a course so large that players had to shout to one another. It was complete with sand traps, bunkers, a rough and was edged with a metal retaining rim to keep the grass from intruding onto the court. Once off the court, a player needed several shots to get back on, including a mild wedge shot to pop the ball over the rim. Once Swope ordered his partner, after a hit shot, to "destroy" the other ball by driving it off the court. When his partner started to protest, Swope roared: "Don't argue with me, dammit, do as I say."

Properly cowed, his partner followed instructions, and blasted the ball off the court and down the road leading to Long Island Sound. "Good work," said Swope, approvingly. Suddenly he did a double-take and screamed, "Good God, that was my ball!"

Swope was a true croquet maven, and Harpo recalls a match that he and Swope completed while the governor of New York, Al Smith, was kept waiting on the telephone. Another time it became too dark to continue a match, but Swope had his guests ring the court with their cars and turn the lights on. The game was completed, but five cars had dead batteries as a result.

Another croquet aficionado was Averell Harriman. During a Thanksgiving party a snow storm came up while a game was in progress. Rather than stop the match, he hired eight men, complete with snow plows, shovels and a tractor, to clean the course. And the game went on. Harriman had to make many sacrifices in the service of his country, but one thing he never gave up was his love of croquet. While ambassador to Russia, he demanded that the Soviets set up a croquet court for his use. Later, serving as Secretary of Commerce, he was in San Francisco on business and called Darryl F. Zanuck to bemoan the fact that he hadn't been able to play croquet for a week. "Why you poor fellow," sympathized Zanuck, "fly down to Palm Springs." Harriman arrived at 11 p.m. and the two played on the lighted court until four in the morning. A tired but satisfied Harriman then boarded a plane for Washington.

Zanuck, known in croquet circles as "the terrible-tempered Mr. Bang" for his aggressive style of play, was probably the main reason croquet became popular in Hollywood after the Second World War. As Moss Hart said, "Zanuck has the true croquet spirit. He trusts no one but himself; never concedes—no matter how far behind he may be—and he hates his opponents with an all-enduring hate."

Zanuck had constructed a magnificent 80′ by 82′ croquet court in Hollywood that was complete with a water hazard. Upkeep alone in those pre-inflation days was $14,000 a year, and stakes on some of the matches were reported to be as high as $10,000 a game. Among the notables who played there were Tyrone Power, Howard Hawkes, Mike Romanoff, George Sanders and Louis Jourdan. Another regular was Gregory Ratoff, the Russian actor and impresario, who was so fat he played with the mallet held under

Darryl F. Zanuck's home croquet course.

his arm.

Louis Jourdan was by far the best player, due in part to his exposure to the subtleties of the British game. It was not unusual for him to go around the course in one turn, and he was said to be accurate on shots up to 100 feet. When Sam Goldwyn built two courses in Beverly Hills, George Sanders suggested sand traps for the main court to stop Jourdan but "it only slowed him up about ten minutes." Today Jourdan is still a first class player but, as one wag commented, "Louis never really gained his confidence on the croquet court until after making GIGI."

Another Hollywood player was actor Gig Young who, during one match, was faced with a very difficult shot. The course, situated near the San Andreas fault, was shaken by a tremor that caused everyone to run for cover. Upon returning to the court, it was discovered that Young's ball was now in a perfect position to run the hoop. Gig smiled and commented wryly, "It must have been an act of God."

Although there was a great deal of croquet interest in Hollywood during the 40's, the Eastern players still considered themselves the best. To settle the issue, the first and only East-West championship was held in 1946. Over 300 Hollywood names, including Clifton Webb, Douglas Fairbanks and Howard Hughes, showed up at Hawkes' ranch in Palm Springs for the crucial match.

The East squad of Tyrone Power and agent Fefe Ferry was led by Moss Hart, while the West was represented by Zanuck—as captain, of course—and Howard Hawkes. Hart was more careful in this match than he had been the previous summer when he had attempted to whack an opponent's ball into the next county and hit his foot instead, spending six weeks on crutches.

Alexander Woollcott: "Irascible in victory, impossible in defeat."

The West won the first match but, even with Zanuck protesting every shot, the East came back to win the second game and set up the all-important rubber game. By the time the third match was to be played it was evening, and the lights had to be turned on. One critical play occurred during the game when Tyrone Power had to drive Zanuck's ball as far as possible. Hart sidled up and whispered, "Remember *'Daytime Wife,'* a turkey produced by Zanuck starring Power. Properly aroused, Tyrone sent the ball winging. A turning point occurred when Zanuck flubbed a shot early in the match and someone in the crowd yelled, "Well, that's one shot he can't retake." Zanuck never did identify the culprit, but his game was off and the East went on to win the third match.

The three games lasted a total of 11 hours and, toward the end, things did get a bit loose. As Hart put it, "Cheating is as much a part of croquet as it is of poker, but in the dark it got out of control." Nonetheless, the winning East team complained bitterly about the size of the victor's cup, which was hardly visible to the naked eye.

Although Zanuck is a serious croquet player, some frivolity does creep into his game. When someone new was introduced to the game at his place in Palm Springs, they were given "the ball" to use. This was a ball that looked like any other ball but was canted to roll every way but straight. Mike Romanoff, a good and good-natured croquet player, was the butt of several of Zanuck's practical jokes. "We gave Romanoff a ball once that was painted just like a grapefruit. Then he hit it under a tree with a lot of real grapefruits lying around. He went around there for twenty minutes whacking the hell out of real grapefruit. He was absolutely drenched with grapefruit juice."

Zanuck has another favorite Romanoff story as well. "Then there's 'the mallet'. It's my personal mallet I tell Romanoff, and I want him to have it because it's so delicately balanced it will make a crack player out of him—finest wood from the Himalayas and absolutely without price. Only, for God's sake, under no circumstances is he to lay it down or throw it away.

"Well, of course, it's a breakaway mallet and along about the third swing the thing falls into splinters. Of course, the boob is white-faced and I'm having a stroke. I fall to the ground and wail, 'it's irreplaceable, the mallet's irreplaceable'."

In the late fifties and until his death, one of the most hallowed croquet grounds in America were the two courts at Sam Goldwyn's Beverly Hills estate. Along with the other Hollywood regulars mentioned above Goldwyn would play for hours on end with visiting East Coast aficionados' such as TV Producer William O. Harback, Nick Vanoff and authors Peter Maas and George Plimpton. Mrs. Goldwyn was finally compelled to abolish play on the courts just before Sam's death because he would get overly excited in his bedroom listening to the sound of mallets hitting balls while friends were playing below the window.

Meanwhile, in the East, croquet was entering a new and vigorous era. Centering in the Long Island South Shore resort communities of Westhampton Beach and Southampton, two separate groups independently began to form what has become the nucleus of the resurgence and popularity of the game today.

By 1966, the Americans had progressed far enough to send a three man team consisting of Homer Landon, Henri White, and Walter Margulies against the Hurlingham Croquet Club in England, an example of enthusiasm triumphing over experience. Hurlingham, which has seven croquet courts, has over 1000 members and is to croquet what Wimbledon (once known as the Wimbledon Croquet and Tennis Club) is to tennis. The American squad was soundly thrashed in its first venture into international competition, but the players learned many valuable tips and points of strategy. As one Londoner remarked airily, "You Americans play a primitive croquet, the kind we used to play 50 years ago."

Undaunted, the Americans issued a challenge the following year, and this time the British team journeyed to New York to play at the Westhampton Mallet Club. This time the match was played under American nine-wicket rules, and the games ended in a three-to-three tie.

The series went back to Hurlingham in 1968, and, playing under British rules, the Americans were soundly defeated 8 to 0.

Croquet courts based on the English layout (not all, but many of putting green quality) have been put down in Long Island, New York, Palm Beach, Bermuda and California. Clubs from these areas have painstakingly (and sometimes painfully) adapted, modified, and amended local rule variations into the American six-wicket croquet game. These clubs, as the founding members of The United States Croquet Association, have adopted them for their own and inter-club tournament play. During this period, more and more Americans and their neighbors in Bermuda and Jamaica have taken up the game in earnest, with top players reaching levels of skill formidable enough to challenge our English friends on their own grounds as well as here in the U.S.

Although American six-wicket rules do now and will probably continue to differ from the Laws of the British Association, the U.S.C.A. is confident that Americans practicing the British style will expand their shot-making skills and their ultimate enjoyment of croquet.

*Croquet seems to have been evolved by
some process of nature, as a crystal forms
or a flower grows—perfect, in accordance
with eternal laws.*
　　—Newport Croquet Club rules, 1867

# IV
# Beginning Play

Croquet is probably America's most misunderstood sport. People picture croquet players as sedentary types who haphazardly tap balls around a lawn, using childish mallets, flimsy wire wickets and a couple of wooden stakes. The game is considered to provide neither the mental stimulation of chess, nor the physical challenge of tennis.

Croquet is, in fact, a grueling and uncompromising sport, one which demands skill, intelligence, control and stamina. Likening serious croquet to the familiar "backyard" version is like comparing the New York Mets to your child's Little League team.

To start with, the equipment used in competitive croquet is much more business-like: heftier mallets; larger balls; and, in place of the thin wire hoops, heavy, rather formidable cast iron or aluminum wickets—with a clearance only one-eighth of an inch wider than the balls. And in place of the typical nine-wicket layout we all grew up with, there is the more challenging six-wicket layout, with one lone stake in the middle. This six-wicket layout is used in all international competition and in all U.S. Croquet Association tournaments, while the nine-wicket, "bust 'em into the next county" game has been relegated to the backyard.

Most of the points discussed in the following chapters can be applied to both the nine-wicket and six-wicket games. Running a wicket or executing a split shot is the same whatever the game, and you will find as you read through the rules that there are fewer differences between the two than might be thought. So when we talk about croquet in this book, we are referring to the standard six-wicket game and, unless noted, not the nine-wicket version. Make sure you understand the chapter on principles of play and the chapter on the court layout; these will give you general background before you forge ahead to the challenge of croquet.

*As each player goes through the first hoop, as he undergoes a metamorphosis ... The male antagonist becomes a creature too vile for language, the decency of womanhood has disappeared by the third hoop."*
—*Living Age,* circa 1898

*In croquet as it should be played, there is no such thing as a 'careful' player or a 'forward' player. Both are fools.*
—B.L.J. Tollemache, *Croquet*

# V
# Basic Principles of Play

American croquet, unlike the British version, is a sequence game, i.e. the blue, red, black and yellow balls are hit in successive turns. The British game is non-sequence; a player could elect to hit the blue ball (assuming, in singles, he is playing blue and black) on several successive turns. The object of the game is to score more points than your opponent, by hitting your two balls through a course of six wickets twice and, finally, against a center peg. Each ball must run each wicket in the proper sequence and from the appropriate direction. The winner is the player(s) who makes a circuit of the course first with both balls or, in a time-limit game, the side with the greatest number of points when time is called.

The proper direction of play is as follows: first go through the four outside hoops, then hoops five and six in the center. These wickets are then scored in the opposite direction; the second wicket becomes 1-back (the seventh wicket you must run), the first wicket becomes 2-back and so on.

Each wicket, or hoop-stop, made in the proper order by each ball is worth 1 point, as is the peg, for a total of 13 points. Thus a side of one or two players can score a maximum of 26 points. In recording results, the full scores are usually given (e.g., 26–14, 26–9), although sometimes the difference between the game scores of the players is given (a shutout is recorded as + or − 26).

Croquet is a game of alternating turns. In doubles matches, the ball assigned on the first stroke must be the one used throughout the match. In singles matches, the striker alternates balls but the ball that a player starts with on a particular turn must be played for the duration of the turn.

Play is made in croquet by hitting a ball with a mallet. The person doing this is called the striker. A turn is one stroke, but extra strokes may be earned in two ways. One way is by running a hoop in the proper order. This earns one "continuation" stroke. The second method is by making a roquet—hitting another ball with your own. This entitles you to a "croquet" shot and a continuation shot. While this is the general rule, you should note the following exceptions: First, once you have roqueted a ball, you are said to be 'dead' on that ball, and cannot hit it again until you have gone through your next wicket. Second, if a wicket is run during a croquet shot, the extra continuation stroke is forfeited. A player can never earn more than one croquet and one continuation stroke on any one shot. Third, hoop strokes are not cumulative. If you run two wickets, or hoops, on the same stroke—possible, but exceptionally rare—you still earn only one continuation stroke. If you run all the wickets in a single turn you have achieved an "all-round break", croquet's equivalent of a no-hitter.

At the game's opening each side chooses for the starting order by flipping a coin. One side takes the red and yellow balls, the other blue and black. To start the game, the first striker plays the blue ball onto the course from a point a mallet's length in back of the first wicket. When the starting player's turn ends, his opponent, playing the red ball, begins, and the sequence continues until all four balls are entered into play. All balls are dead on each other until they have made the first wicket, so no real strategy occurs until the first hoop has been run. If all players but one make the first hoop, they are still dead on that player's ball until he has successfully run the hoop. This is true in singles as well as doubles.

In regulation croquet, when a ball is sent out of bounds, it is replaced at the sideline, a mallet's head in from where it left the course. If you ricochet your own ball off the course on a roquet shot there is no penalty. Your ball is replaced at the proper spot, and your continuation shot follows. You may not, however, knock a roqueted ball over the line without ending your turn. If you do hit another ball over the line (on a roquet or croquet shot), the balls are replaced one mallet head in from where they went out.

No further discussion of balls out of bounds can be made without explaining the situation known as being "in hand." This refers to balls that have to be lifted and repositioned during a turn. This arises when a ball lies on the boundary line within a mallet's head of the line, or has gone over the line. If two or more balls have to be replaced, the opponent determines the order of their repositioning.

A player may lift and reposition in four other instances. Of course, one must lift a ball after a roquet in order to take croquet. Sometimes balls must be replaced after a fault or irregularity has

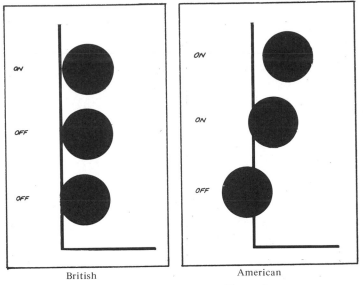

British           American

When a ball is out of bounds.

occurred. A ball that has not made the No. 1 wicket may be lifted to clear a path for another ball, but it must be replaced. Lastly, if a player finds his ball wired from all alive balls, he is permitted to lift his ball and place it in contact with any one of those balls and take croquet. "Wired" refers to a ball that cannot be roqueted due to obstruction by a wicket, stake or dead ball.

Although it has been explained in passing, it should be emphasized that being dead on one or more balls drastically affects play and strategy. You cannot hit a ball you are dead on until you have 'cleaned' yourself by clearing the next wicket. The penalty for hitting a dead ball is ending your turn, and the return of the balls to their original position. It is crucial not to become dead on multiple balls unless you are reasonably sure of running a wicket on your continuation shot. Being dead on several balls obviously limits your break and roquet-making abilities, and, hence, the duration of your turn. You should therefore plan ahead, weigh the potential gain or loss of each shot, and try to assure yourself the free use of all the balls. If you commit the error of becoming dead on two or three balls you can be sure your opponent will try to keep you in that position for as long as possible. Whenever you are in position to run your proper wicket and clean yourself of any deadness, your opponent will attempt to knock you away. As Darryl

Zanuck put it, "when you're three ball dead, you're just a useless bum."

Conversely, it is to your advantage to keep your opponent from cleaning himself of any deadness. In some instances, when your opponent is "live" on your ball you might tempt him into hitting it, thereby making him dead on that ball.

It is imperative, in quality play at any level, to be aware of the status of each ball in the match. You should know which ball is the most advanced, which balls are alive, which are dead for each player, and which wickets each player is going for. Be especially aware of the playing order of each ball. Before sending a ball to a spot, review which ball will be shot next.

You will find that the tactics you adopt are determined by a variety of factors: the situation in hand, the quality of your opponent's play, your own abilities, the state of the game, and the court conditions. As you become more experienced, you will find that your tactics change from game to game as these variables change.

Generally speaking, it is best to play in a manner somewhere between angelic caution and foolish aggression. You should play it safe, if necessary, to prevent yourself from getting into an unfavorable position. Do not, however, in easing your own position, set your opponent up for a potentially damaging shot. Defensive play is also a big factor; cases will arise when you can block your foes' progress by strategic placement of your own balls.

These are just some of the basic principles of the game, and a few of the beginning strategies and tactics. Other points, as well as some of the more advanced techniques, will be touched upon in later chapters. But this review should give you an idea of some of the complexities involved in croquet as it is seriously played. It is a very different game as played under the rules of the United States Croquet Association, from the brand of croquet found in most back yards. Adopting some or all of the rules and recommendations in this book should greatly enhance the pleasure you get from the sport.

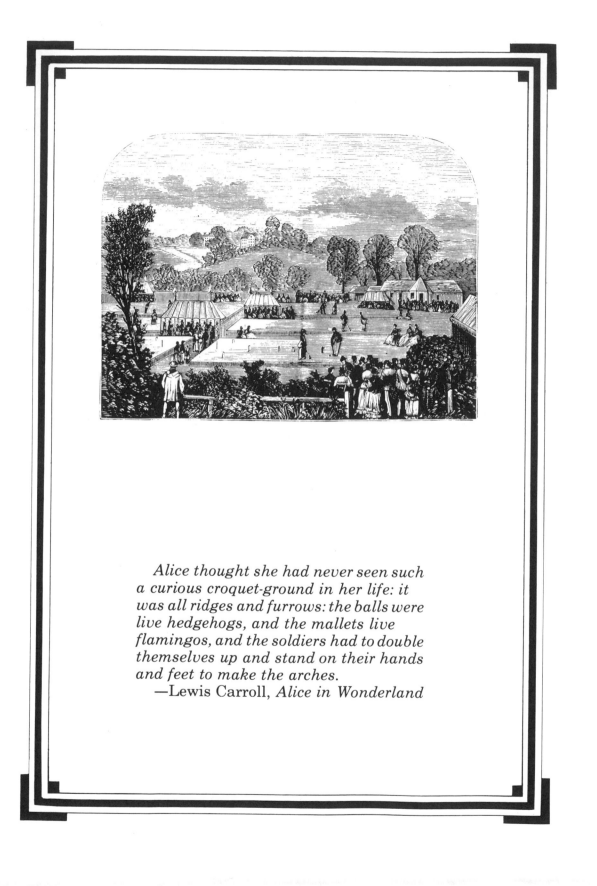

Alice thought she had never seen such
a curious croquet-ground in her life: it
was all ridges and furrows: the balls were
live hedgehogs, and the mallets live
flamingos, and the soldiers had to double
themselves up and stand on their hands
and feet to make the arches.
—Lewis Carroll, *Alice in Wonderland*

# VI
# Court and Equipment

The standard American six-wicket croquet court, that used for tournament play, is a rectangle measuring 105 by 84 feet. If available space is too small for a full sized court, a proportionately smaller rectangle can be used, so long as the ratio of the sides is five to four. The boundaries of the court should be clearly marked. The inside edge of the border is the actual boundary line. The four corners of the court are known respectively as corners 1,2,3, and 4, and the boundaries are designated South, West, North and East, regardless of the geographical orientation of the court. Within this rectangle, the six wickets and one stake are laid out, with the stake placed at the intersection of the two diagonals. The corner wickets, known as the outer hoops, are set with their centers 21 feet from their adjacent boundaries. The center wickets, or inner hoops, are placed 21 feet from the stake. Of course, if your court is smaller than the standard size, the wickets should be arranged proportionately. Local conditions may require other layouts, but 50 x 40 feet is generally considered the minimum size for croquet.

Many players in the United States, especially backyard players, use a layout of nine wickets and two stakes, with one stake used as a starting and finishing peg, and the wickets laid out in a double diamond. Since there are few regulation courts in America, and since the game is often played in back yards and other available space, the size of the courts often varies considerably. Preferably, the court is placed on a flat, closely-cropped lawn, with the length twice the width, but many players incorporate hills, trees, streams, and other natural and man-made hazards into their courses.

The dimensions of the British standard court are the same as the American. There is, however, an unmarked inner rectangle one yard inside the court called the yard line. On each of the short sides of the yard line are other unmarked lines called baulk lines. The one on the bottom or south yard line extends from the west corner to the center of the yard line, and the one on the north side goes from the

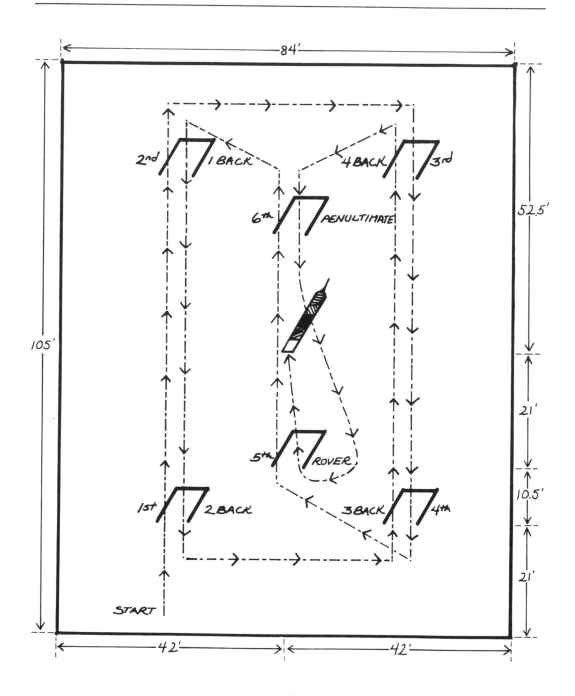

**Official United States Croquet Association 6-wicket layout with direction of play.**

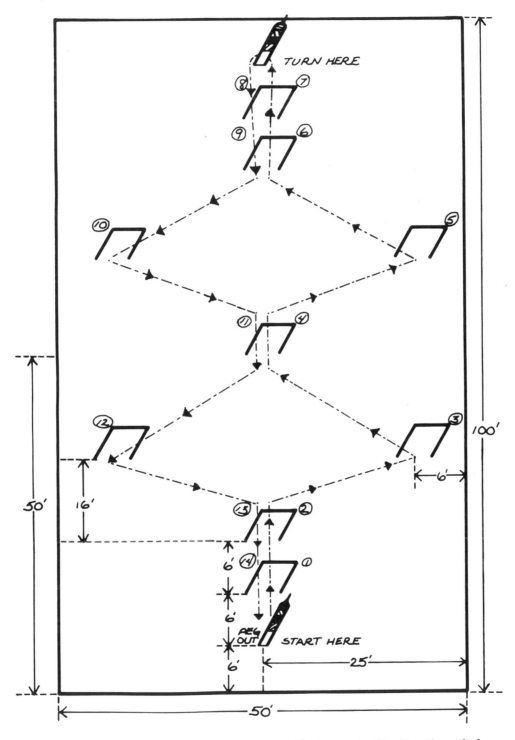

TURN HERE

START HERE

PEG OUT

**Official United States Croquet Association 9-wicket layout with direction of play.**

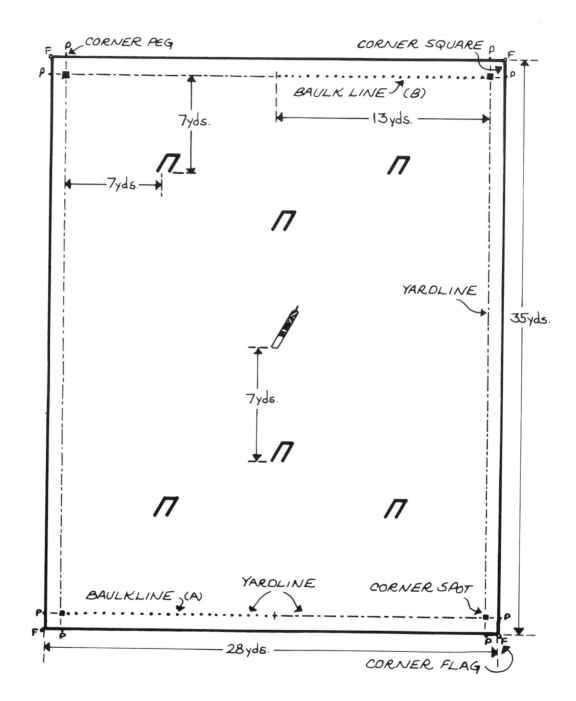

**Standard British 6-wicket layout.**

center of the yard line to the east corner. All the hoops are placed parallel to the north and south boundaries. In the American game, the rover wicket is played pointing inwards to the stake, the major difference between the two settings.

## EQUIPMENT

*"There are really two great moments for a croquet player, aside from winning a game. The first is when he is introduced to croquet. The second is when he feels he is good enough to order his own mallet with his initials on top of the handle."*
—Peter Maas

Mallets, wickets, and balls, along with stakes and a few accessories used for guidance and keeping track of the play, comprise the basic equipment necessary to play croquet. The mallet is the most important piece of equipment and will be discussed last. Most casual players in this country have used the rounded, flexible wire hoops that come with most garden sets. The official wickets are quite different. They are made of rounded iron 5/8 of an inch in diameter and are of uniform thickness. They are solid and not at all

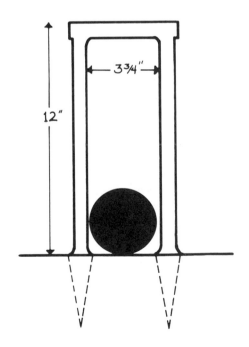

An official hoop. Note the clips used to mark the progress of each ball.

**A standard wicket, with, at right, a winter wicket. Note the thinner uprights of the winter hoop.**

flexible. There should be a foot clearance between the top of the crown of the wicket and the ground. The crown is straight and at right angles to the uprights. The distance between the uprights must not be less than 3 11/16th inches or more than four inches. The distance between the uprights should be uniform for the entire wicket. All the wickets are painted white, but the crown of the first wicket is painted blue, that of the last or "rover" painted red. The wickets, of course, should be firmly fixed in the ground. There is another, lighter form of wicket usually referred to as winter wickets, because they are more easily placed in the hard, frozen ground. They are 7/16ths of an inch in diameter, with the same clearance as regular hoops. They are used in non-tournament games as the conditions warrant.

The stake is made of wood and is 18 inches above the ground. It is painted white, with blue, red, black, and yellow bands descending in that order from the top. The stake must be vertical and firmly planted in the ground. Some stakes have an extension attached to the top to hold the clips. There are four clips, one the color of each ball, and they are used in play to designate to the players the progress of the respective balls. They are placed on the crown of the next hoop in sequence for the initial six wickets, and on the upright of each wicket for the return six. They are attached to the stake extension when a player is going for the peg.

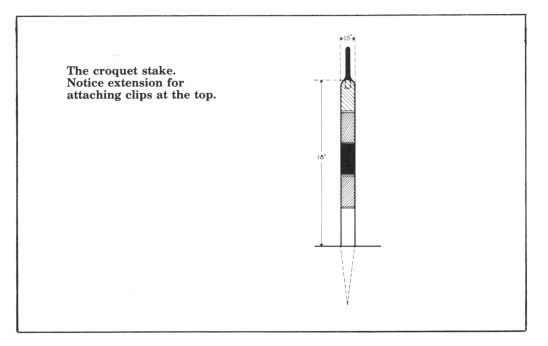

The croquet stake. Notice extension for attaching clips at the top.

The four croquet balls are colored, respectively, blue, red, black, and yellow, and are usually made of wood or composite. Other materials may be used as long as they are consistent. All the balls must weight the same, and their weight must be between 15 3/4 ounces and 16 1/4 ounces. Their diameter must be 3 5/8 inches. This leaves a clearance between ball and wicket of between 1/16 and 3/8 of an inch. This, obviously, is very small indeed, and makes accuracy extremely important. Corner pegs and corner flags, which serve to delineate the corner squares, make up the rest of the court equipment.

## Mallets

The mallet is the only piece of croquet equipment that the player can choose to his liking. Since you do have a choice, it is best to take your time, look around, and try a few before you pick. There is a large range of equipment available in all price ranges and qualities, from inexpensive garden sets to custom made mallets costing hundreds of dollars. Serious players have for years ordered theirs from John Jaques of Surrey, England. Jaques equipment is available from a number of stores in the United States, or can be ordered directly from the USCA.

Placing a clip, in the 19th century. At the height of croquet's popularity, candle sockets were attached to the wicket for night play.

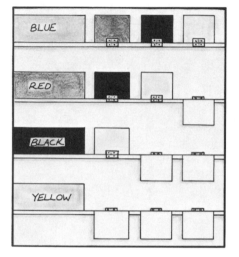

A deadness board. Note that blue is 3-ball dead.

There are no weight or size restrictions on mallets. Years ago, the tendency was toward the heavier mallet, but today most weigh around three pounds, with three pounds, nine ounces considered heavy. The shaft of the mallet is usually about three feet long, and the shorter Irish style mallets about two feet eight inches long. As a general rule, a shorter shaft gives a player greater freedom of movement, while a longer one provides greater steadiness. The shaft is most commonly made of ash, although hickory and Malacca cane are also used. Cane shafts are the springiest, and hickory, although more subject to warpage than the others, probably provides the best combination of strength and spring. The grip area on the shaft is frequently bound with cork, string, or even a golf grip. Non-slipping suede can also be used. Most mallets have octagonal grips, but oval grips are also used.

The head of the mallet must be wood, but metal may be used for weighting or strengthening. Lignum vitae and boxwood are the most common mallet-head materials. Lignum vitae tends to be brittle, so heads of this wood should be brass bound. The heads may be round, or square and flat-bottomed. The square type is most popular in Australia, while the cylindrical style is favored in Britain. Both are popular in the U.S. They work equally well, so the choice is largely a matter of personal taste.

The balancing point of the mallet should be about 1/5 of the distance from the bottom of the head to the top of the shaft. It is a good idea not to buy any extra shaft that isn't handled. Shorter shafts may be ordered, or you can cut it down from the top, but be *very* careful or the balance of the mallet will be destroyed. Make sure that the shaft is straight and the hole in the head for the shaft is accurately bored. The Rev. Elvey, a former president of the British Croquet Council, suggests that it is good to have the grain of the shaft at a 90° angle to the head or exactly parallel to the head. This can offset warpage. If your mallet gets wet, always dry it off before you store it. You can use varnish or shellac for weatherproofing. When your mallet is not in use, hang it upside down between two pegs. Don't store it in a corner, as this will put the handle out of proper alignment. And *never* use your mallet for any purpose other than its proper one. With decent care, a quality mallet can last a lifetime.

**A croquet still-life. Note the different mallet-head styles.**

*The British form of croquet is a better
game than ours . . . more sportsman-like.
Ours is a more strategic game and far more
emotional. In our game you do what you
call 'destroying' your opponent. The
British don't go so far. They wouldn't think
of doing things like some of our former
leaders, like the late Alexander Woollcott.
Why, he had his court beside a lake and
thought nothing of knocking a guest's ball
in the water. That sometimes caused
trouble.*

—Averell Harriman

# VII
# American vs. British Rules and Styles of Play

British croquet is as different from American croquet as cricket is from baseball. Like many American customs, croquet rules in the United States were originally based on the game played by our British cousins, but as the English game evolved, Yankee ingenuity (or an historic disregard for the way it's done elsewhere) refused to adapt to this evolution and brought about subtle and not so subtle changes in American croquet rules. Perhaps the American temperament is less to blame than the fact that as house lots became smaller in our growing land, the luxury of a regulation British court (eighty four by one hundred five feet of flat rolled lawn) restricted play to club grounds. Buffs who wished to play or practice on available greens began to improvise, and the inevitable changes or lack of changes were under way.

Croquet games in this country have tended to vary from lawn to lawn, depending essentially on good sportmanship, force of personality and who owns the lawn. The movie mogul Sam Goldwyn is less known in croquet circles for his often quoted malaprops than for the fact that he installed a sandtrap on his court expressly to thwart the better-playing Louis Jourdan. This rather extreme example of rule flexibility proves the point made by English purists—American variations of the game have diluted it.

Aside from the visual similarity of the court setting there are quite a number of basic differences between croquet as played in Great Britain and either the American six-wicket or nine-wicket versions.

Clearly the most influential of these rules concerns "deadness". In the American game if you acquire "deadness" on any or all balls, you remain dead on them until you have cleared your next wicket. The British game provides that all "deadness" is cleared at the beginning of that ball's next turn, regardless of whether or not it has cleared its hoop.

The net effect of this difference is the greater emotional strain and thus more conservative nature of the American player facing the almost terminal condition of being "three ball dead" throughout the game. His English cousin may feel free to attempt more venturesome shots (and with this practice become more skillful at them) with less pressure or traumatic concern since he will be "alive" one way or another during his next turn.

Major layout changes are the invisible "yard line" set inside all boundary lines and two Baulk lines running one half the width of the South (from #1 corner) and North (from #3 corner) boundary lines in the English game. The Baulk areas are used to begin the game from any part thereof and to play legally lifted balls in hand from (after being wired or shot in during an English Advanced game).

In the American layout the yard line is reduced to a mallet-head (9″) and there are no baulk lines designated or used.

Other rules that tend to provide the English with the advantage of a looser, more wide-open game than the American versions are:

### Rotation

*(English:)*  Non-rotation play of either ball on a side during that sides turn. (Can decide pace of each ball's advance.)

*(American:)*  Must play in rotation or sequence. (Causes better player to have to advance faster than weaker partner.)

### Roquet
### (out of bounds)

*(English:)*  May roquet or rush a ball out-of-bounds and continue to play it.

*(American:)*  Turn ends. (Ball usually ends up next to another ball which, if an opponent's ball, gives advantage to him.)

### Bisques

*(English:)*  An English bisque is an additional shot from where the ball ends *after* a stroke.

*(American:)*  An American bisque shot is an additional shot from where the ball started before the stroke.

### Out of Bounds

*(English:)*  Ball out of bounds is replaced one yard in bounds.

48

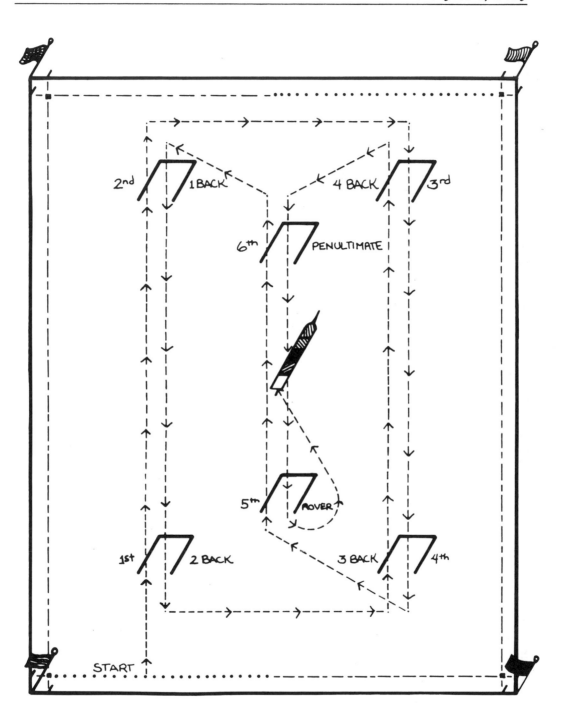

British direction of play.

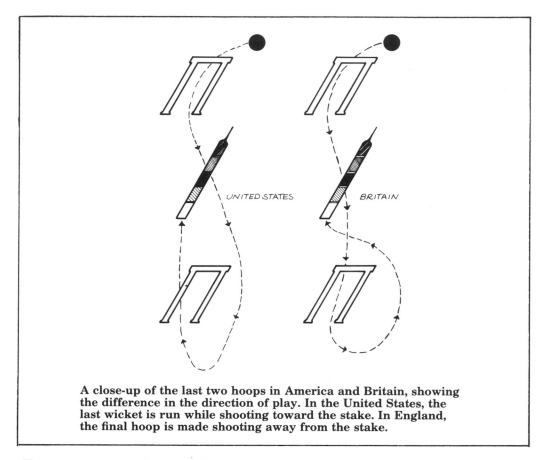

**A close-up of the last two hoops in America and Britain, showing the difference in the direction of play. In the United States, the last wicket is run while shooting toward the stake. In England, the final hoop is made shooting away from the stake.**

(Easier to approach and provides better shot angles.)
*(American:)* One mallet-head in.

Other differences which conversely provide somewhat more difficult moments for the English are:

### Rover Wicket
*(English:)* Rover Hoop must be run going away from stake.
*(American:)* Rover wicket run inward toward stake. (Easier to stake out or clean deadness on ball for rover from this direction.)

### Opening
### (start of game)
*(English:)* Opening strokes of game are taken from either Baulk line (never stroked directly to No. 1 wicket) and balls are "alive" on all others after first stroke.

*(American:)* Begin game from one yard in front of wicket No. 1. (Balls are not alive until clearing No. 1 wicket.)

## Time Limits

*(English:)* No time regulations for length of game or time between shots.

*(American:)* In USCA tournaments, a maximum of 1½ hours is allowed per match. There is also a 45 second limit between shots.

## Summary: (U.S. vs. British)

The American six-wicket game is a more conservative, but nonetheless as interesting and challenging a game as the English. It places a greater premium on the strategically complex aspects of remembering deadness, rotation sequences, and assessing the strengths and weakness of the opponents than the British game.

The British, capitalizing on their less constricting rules, have thus been able to emphasize, and practice under game conditions, their shot-making skills. That is not to imply that the English game requires less strategy, but rather that it is a strategy more concerned with employing shooting strengths than the more conservative strategy of the Americans.

*The chief difficulty Alice found at first was managing her flamingo: she succeeded in getting its body tucked away, comfortable enough, under her arm, with its legs hanging down, but generally, just as she had got its neck nicely straightened out, and was going to give the hedgehog a blow with its head, it would twist itself around and look up at her, with such a puzzled expression that she could not help bursting out laughing; and, when she had got its head down, and was going to begin again, it was very provoking to find that the hedgehog had unrolled itself, and was in the act of crawling away: besides all this, there was generally a furrow or ridge in the way wherever she wanted to send the hedgehog to, and, as the double up soldiers were always getting up and walking off to other parts of the ground, Alice came to the conclusion that it was a very difficult game indeed.*

—Lewis Carroll, *Alice In Wonderland*

# VIII
# Grips, Stances and the Swing

## The Grip

There are essentially two ways to grip the croquet mallet. The most widely used method is called the reverse palm grip. With this grip, the palm of the upper hand faces the body, and that of the lower hand faces away from the body. The other widely used grip is called the Irish grip, which originated with the great Irish players at the turn of the century, such as Duff Matthews and Cyril Corbally. This grip has both palms facing away from the body. There are some variations of these two basic grips with interlocking or overlocking fingers. Most American players tend to separate their hands and move the lower hand down the shaft toward the head of the mallet. This is called the American style, and it is probably used because of the generally more rugged terrain of American courts, which require more leverage in the stroke than the smoother-surfaced English courts. British players usually keep their hands together close to the top of the mallet shaft, although many players, both British and American, employ both styles in the course of a game.

Comfort and success are the major factors in deciding which grip to use. The most important thing to remember is to have both hands working in concert, with neither hand gaining the mastery over the other. The type of shot you are attempting will also influence your choice of grip.

## The Stance

There are three basic playing stances in croquet. In the oldest style, the golf style, you stand sideways to the object ball (the ball you are going to hit) and swing your mallet across your body like a golf club. Although you have good control with this stance, most of this advantage is lost by the added difficulty in aiming. As a result, this style is rarely used in tournament play today, though there are still a few good players, H.O. Hicks among them, who employ it quite effectively. The golf style is often used in garden croquet,

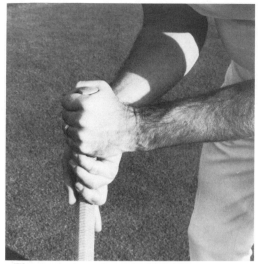

The reverse-palm grip. Also known as the conventional British grip.

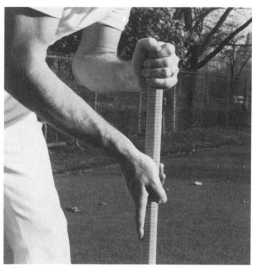

The spread reverse-palm grip. Also known as the conventional American upper grip.

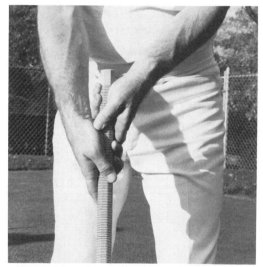

The Irish grip.

Variation of reverse-palm grip.

because of the heavier grass. Because of its similarity to a golf swing, and the shorter mallet used, many Americans find it comfortable and easy to learn.

The two stances most widely used today are the front style and the center style. In the front style, which is also known as the upright style, you face the object ball and swing the mallet outside your feet. This stance allows for more freedom of movement and power than other stances, but it is more difficult to master. It also has the disadvantage that you are not hitting from directly behind the ball. You must guard against the tendency to swing around your body rather than directly towards the ball. You must take care to see that one hand does not predominate over the other. The front style requires a longer mallet than the center style, but it is less tiring.

In the center stance, you swing the mallet in pendulum-fashion between the legs. The advantage of this stance is that you stand behind the ball and swing directly in the line of aim. You must be careful in this stance to see that neither foot predominates. If that does happen, it can cause shots to miss to one side. The center style also requires more wrist control than the other stances.

The golf style.

The side style.

The Irish style is a variation of the center stance. The stance is basically the center stance with a shorter mallet and the Irish grip. The fingers should either overlock or interlock. Some players, 1974 and 1975 British Open Champion Nigel Aspinall among them, feel that the Irish style gives an advantage for longer shots. All are agreed that it is the most physically demanding of the playing styles.

The side style, from the side.

Front view of the center stance, with uneven weight distribution.

The center stance, with even weight distribution.

The center stance, with uneven weight distribution.

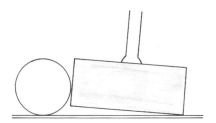

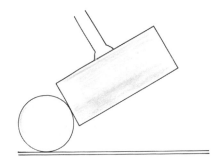

Standing too far from the ball will cause you to swing up at contact.

Standing too close to the ball will cause you to swing down at contact.

## The Swing

One of the most difficult things to learn in the game of croquet is to hit the ball in the correct way. The first thing you must do before hitting the ball is to make sure your shot is lined up properly. In order to do this, you should walk up from behind the ball in the direction you wish to send it. This is called "stalking" the ball. Remember that the aim of the ball is determined not by the mallet but by the relation of your shoulders to the object ball. Once you have stalked the ball and adopted a comfortable stance, bring the mallet back slowly and begin your swing. Hold the mallet firmly, and bring it back pendulum-fashion from the mallet-head, not the top of the shaft. The swing should be flat and from the shoulders, with arms and mallet moving as one. The wrists should be flexible. The rest of your body should NEVER move during the swing. Make sure your head is immobile, as in a golf swing, and keep your eyes on the back of the ball, at the spot where you want to hit it. You should generally try to hit the ball about one inch from the bottom of the mallet-face. Keep your eyes down until the ball is well under way. It is important not to be led by your mallet in the swing, but, in Lord Tollemache's words, "to carry the mallet through." The hands and arms must control the mallet, although, again, it is swung from the shoulders. If too much wrist is used, a badly hit ball will result.

A flatter swing, when the pendulum is from the shoulders, produces a longer follow through, and results in a more accurate shot. If you find that your shot bumps at the beginning, you are probably standing too close to the ball. If it wanders from a straight line, you are standing too far away. And remember, the ball should be swept rather than hit in a definite direction. With practice, you should be able to develop a swing that is both comfortable and accurate.

ROQUER ET CROQUER.

ROQUER ET CROQUER.

*Holding his mallet low and daintily swinging it between his parted spindly legs,... Pnin foreshadowed every stroke with nimble aim-taking oscillations of the mallet head, then gave the ball an accurate tap, and forthwith, still hunched, and with the ball still rolling, walked rapidly to the spot where he had planned for it to stop.*
—V. Nabokov, *Pnin*

# IX
# *Shots*

## Roquet Shot

The basic shot for starting and continuing your turn is the roquet or hit shot. A roquet shot is hitting any of the other three balls (on which you are alive) with your own ball, thereby gaining two extra strokes. After you have roqueted another ball, you move your ball next to the one that has been struck (never the other way around). Then take the first of your two extra shots. This first shot is called the croquet or drive shot, and is taken with your ball touching the roqueted ball. You used to be allowed to place your ball a mallet's head away from the roqueted ball and take your croquet shot from there, but this is no longer permitted.

The second of the two strokes you earn by making a roquet is called a continuation shot. You may use this shot to run a wicket, make another roquet, or, simply, to improve your position. The strategic aspects of the croquet shot and continuation shot will be dealt with later. The proper way to hit a roquet shot is to imagine a straight line between the center of your ball and the center of the ball you wish to hit. Line the shot up by walking up to the ball from behind and getting a "line of aim" on the target ball. This is called "stalking" the ball, and is done the same way you would line up a putt in golf.

Many factors will determine how hard you are going to stroke your shot. If you are aiming at your teammate's ball you might want to remain very close to it, should you miss, and, therefore, you will want to make a soft shot. On the other hand, the situation might call for you to miss the roquet, and keep right on going as far as possible.

The reasons for unintentionally missing a roquet shot are the same ones that cause a dubbed shot in golf. Looking up when you hit your shot is the main cause of missed roquets. Even experienced players do it, but you've got to try to keep your head down. Another reason for missing roquets is failing to bring your eyes back up from the target ball to your ball after lining up the shot. If you are a back yard player it is best just to try to hit the target ball on your roquet shot, rather than to direct it. As you improve you will be able not only to hit the target ball but also to send it to a desired position. To do this, you will need to master the following shots.

The short rush shot.

## The Rush Shot

This is a roquet or hit shot designed to move the roqueted ball a given distance in a particular direction. Any rush shot shorter than three feet is sometimes called a "short rush," while one longer than three feet or so is called a "long rush". A long rush is a tough shot, and, even on very good lawns it is handled only by the better players. But it is a fundamental part of the game and is essential to becoming a good player.

## Straight Rush

This is a hit shot in which you are attempting to hit the target ball dead on rather than hitting it to one side or the other. On a short straight rush you may want to send the target ball a certain distance, so you will vary the force behind your stroke. You can do this by changing your grip, widening the distance between your hands on the shaft, or lengthening your back stroke. On a long straight rush you should only try to meet the target ball, not to send

60

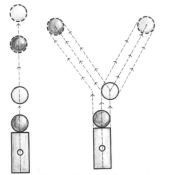

The straight rush and the cut rush.

it a particular distance. If you are attempting to hit the target ball up to a wicket, you should not try a straight rush if this will leave the target ball blocking your hoop. Rather than hitting it straight on, you should hit it slightly off center. Another point to keep in mind is the proper stroke for the lawn conditions. When playing on a rough course, you should hit the ball on the upswing as a precaution against making your ball jump. To hit down on the ball on a rough lawn can prove fatal.

## Cut Rush

This shot is used when you want to drive the target ball to the left or right rather than straight ahead. It is similar to a billiard or pool shot when you are trying to angle a ball into a pocket. In theory, you should not try a cut rush on shots greater than four or five feet but, if the playing surface is even, good players will attempt this shot at two or three times that distance. However, on medium and long range shots, you should try to hit the target ball in the middle rather than cutting it.

## Running The Wicket

The big difference between making a roquet and running a wicket is with the former you are aiming at a solid object and with the latter you are aiming at a space. On a hit shot you can be slightly off and merely tick the target ball, but still, the shot is successful. When shooting for a wicket you don't have quite the same leeway. When shooting for a wicket you should try to visualize a spot right in the middle of the uprights, in the same way a field goal kicker in football would line up his attempt. Of all the basic shots, probably the one most often misplayed is the wicket shot.

**Jack Osborn running a wicket.**

**Approaching the wicket from the side, aim to clear the near upright.**
**Approaching the wicket from straight ahead, aim to go straight through.**

The principles are pretty much the same for the wicket shot as for the roquet shot:

- Do not hurry the back stroke.
- Keep an even back swing.
- Give the mallet head time to swing.

If the ball is in a good position to run the wicket, and you don't need a strong hit, hit true with just a small amount of lift. However, if you are in a good position to run the hoop, but don't want your ball to go too far past it, you should keep the mallet-head as close to the ground as possible and use a slow sweeping motion with no lift. To get the right english on the ball you should hit it at the very top, as if you were breaking an egg.

Remember that it is much easier to approach the wicket from the front, no matter what the distance, than from the side. But if you are to one side of the hoop you should hit the ball as if you are attempting a jump shot. Don't worry if you don't know what a jump shot is—we'll get to that next. If you stroke it correctly the ball will hit the upright and the english will carry it through. It's not an easy shot and virtually impossible if you're playing with flexible wire wickets.

## The Jump Shot

No, this isn't something from the NBA nor is it a shot that you will see in the usual back yard game. A jump shot in croquet is hit like a wedge shot in golf, although you should be careful not to take a divot. Hitting down and behind the ball will cause it to jump. With a little practice you can get quite accurate with the shot.

The jump shot is used when you are unable to make a direct hit on a wicket or ball because one or the other is obstructing your way. Consequently you jump the obstacle.

If you want both your own ball and the target ball to go through the hoop, hit down on the ball but don't overplay it. That way, your ball, instead of making a clean jump, will mount the back of the obstructing ball and both will go through. This is sometimes referred to as the half-jump. In the regular jump shot, your feet should be well in front of the ball, while in the half-jump your feet will not be as far in front.

**A sequence of photos showing the jump shot, which is used when a ball is directly in front of the entrance to the wicket. In this case, only the striker's ball and not the target ball goes through the wicket. With practice, the jump shot can be a very accurate shot and a valuable addition to the croquet player's repertoire.**

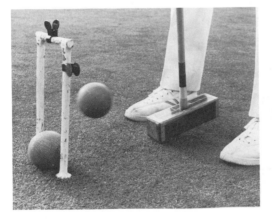

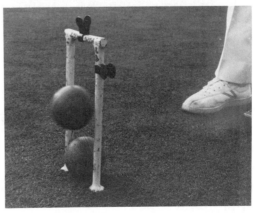

Footing the ball.

## Croquet Shot

As you know, the croquet shot always follows the roquet shot. After you have made your roquet, you move your ball next to the roqueted ball for your croquet shot. In USCA rules and in the British game, the two balls must be touching. The roqueted ball must "rattle" or more, when you take your croquet shot, and you may not touch your ball with hands or feet when making the shot.

This dispenses with the classic backyard move of "footing" your ball when you take croquet. Footing the ball had been outlawed by the British Croquet Association as early as 1870, and the rest of croquet officialdom has now followed suit. Even for the average player this presents no particular problem, although a "footless" croquet shot is less effective in moving the croqueted ball a long distance.

Of perhaps greater consequence is the rule mandating that the two balls must be touching, rather than up to a mallet-head apart, in a croquet shot. This also makes for a tougher and riskier shot.

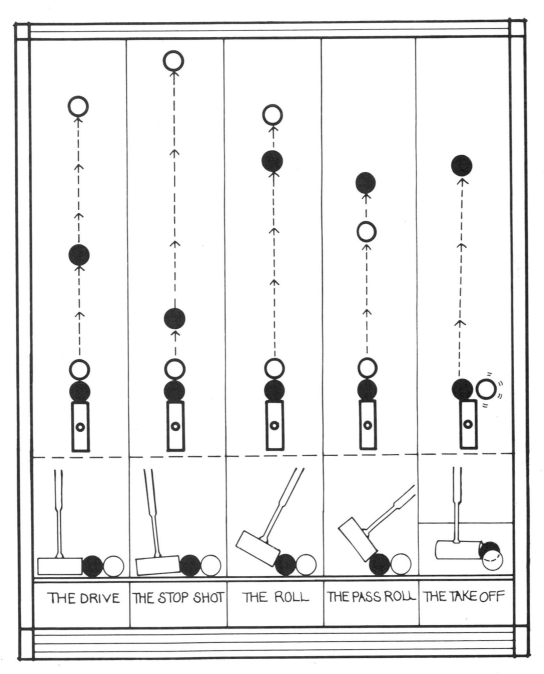

**The basic croquet shots. Note that the balls travel varying distances and that the balls are struck differently.**

There are several basic croquet shots that you should master if you're going to get maximum enjoyment from the sport.

Hitting true, hitting up and hitting
down.

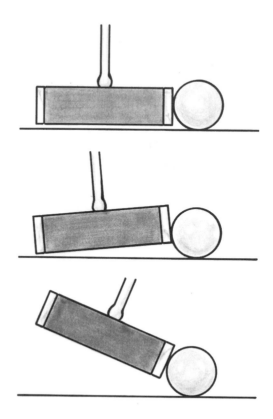

## The Hammer Shot

This is used when you are prevented from swinging your mallet
because the wicket is in the way. Sometimes this shot is even taken
with your back to your ball. It's a tough shot, easy to foul on, so don't
worry about it unless you are a pretty advanced player. If you are
forced to take a hammer shot, remember that, like the jump shot, it
is not necessary to take a divot or otherwise damage the ground
with your follow-through.

## The Drive Shot

The drive is a croquet shot in which you place your ball directly
behind the roqueted ball and hit them both in the same direction.
For this shot you should assume a balanced stance, and hit your
ball with the mallet-head level, using a normal follow-through. Hit
the shot as if there were no other ball in front of yours. The
croqueted ball should travel about three times as far as yours in a
straight line.

The drive shot. The mallet-head is totally level.

## The Roll Shot

In the roll shot, also known as the double roll or trundle, both balls will travel about the same distance, although not necessarily in the same direction. This is a tough shot, and to do it successfully, you should stand well over the two balls and hit down on your swing. The actual stroke is not as much a swing as it is a downward sweep. It is very important to have a follow-through with a roll shot, to give the shot enough push to allow the back ball to catch up with the front ball. If the back ball passes the front ball it is called a "pass roll." Since there is a danger of fouling on the roll shot, you should move your hands apart and keep them in advance of the mallet-head.

## The Stop Shot

The object of the stop shot is to have your ball remain stationary, or travel only a short distance, while the forward ball travels a great distance. The stop shot is one of the easiest of the basic croquet shots. You should stand well back of the two balls, and in the stop shot, unlike the roll shot, you should hit with no follow-through. If played correctly, the front ball should travel up to ten times farther than the back ball. In croquet circles, a long stop shot is known as a "beefy stop shot."

The roll shot. Observe that he is hitting down on the mallet.

The pass roll shot. Note hands and acute angle of the mallet-head.

## The Split Shot

It is obvious that the distance the croqueted ball travels is determined by the angle of the split. The wider the angle, the farther

The stop shot. Note the slightly raised mallet-head.

your own ball travels because you hit less of the croqueted ball. It is very similar to splits in billiards or pool. Decide where you want the croqueted ball to end up and where you want your own ball to go, and the rest is determined by experience. The lines that the two balls will take will form an angle and to complete the split shot successfully you should "split the angle". A soft stroke is used if you want the two balls to travel a short distance, and a harder stroke is taken if you want them to travel farther. In any case, the line of aim that your mallet takes will be the same.

Ninety degrees is the widest angle for a split shot. Trying for any greater angle causes the front ball to travel a shorter distance. Keep in mind that when a split shot is made with a roll shot, there is a tendency for the balls to pull in toward each other. This doesn't occur on a stop shot because of the english used.

Remember, hitting up will decrease the length travelled by your own ball and increase the distance travelled by the forward ball. Hitting down will have the opposite effect.

## The Take Off Shot

This is a variation of the drive shot. The object of the take off shot is to make the ball you hit move only a short distance while your ball goes a long way. To do this correctly, the angle formed by the mallet-head and the two balls must be slightly more than a right angle. If not, the front ball will go much farther than you intended. You should also stand over the two balls and hit down on your shot.

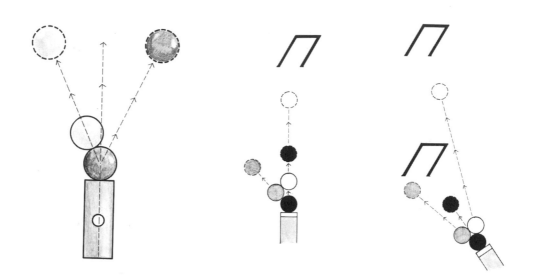

Since the stop shot is easier than the roll shot, you should try to play with a minimum of rolls and a maximum of stops. It is easier said than done, but that should be your goal.

### The Cannon Shot

The cannon shot is a shot involving three balls, and should be used by every player no matter what their level of ability. It is one of the· most neglected shots in croquet, especially by American players.

There are four types of cannon shots:

### The Corner Cannon

This is a combination of the rush and croquet shots and, although called a corner cannon, can be played anywhere on the court. The object of the corner cannon is to send the croqueted ball to a certain spot while at the same time your ball is hitting a third ball. As you can see, the shot can be taken anywhere on the field. Make sure when shooting a corner cannon that you don't knock the other ball out of bounds because if you do, under USCA rules, your turn ends.

Several other cannon shots, with the delightfully British names of Running Cannon, Pseudo Cannon and Kiss Cannon, are explained in the Glossary.

Another group of shots includes those in which the ball is

deliberately bounced off a peg or wicket in order to get a better position or to hit another ball. Since this shot rarely occurs when wire wickets are used, and infrequently even with the heavy iron wickets, we won't go into detail here.

## The Peel

This is a shot which separates the backyard players from the serious players. A peel occurs when you cause a ball other than your own, whether on a roquet or a croquet stroke, to run its proper wicket. The peeled ball gets credit for running the hoop but gets no extra stroke, as would have occurred if the ball had been run on its own. However, if you make a peel on your roquet stroke, you get both a croquet shot and a continuation shot. Usually you would only peel your opponent's ball when you think it is possible to make it a rover, which would allow you to stake him out. If you stake him out, he is left with one ball to negotiate around the course. You must be careful not to get stuck doing the last peel with your own ball once it has become a rover. If you miss, your opponents could turn the tables and peg you out, leaving your partner to fend for himself. This last situation would not occur under British or advanced USCA rules, since only a rover can stake out a rover.

Under American rules, a peel occurs more frequently with your partner's ball than with your opponent's ball. This usually happens when your partner's ball is in the "jaws of the hoop" or is two or three ball dead and unable to roquet another ball. Peeling your partner through his wicket allows him to become alive again on all balls.

In addition to the single peel explained above, there are several other kinds of peels:

*The Double Peel*  This is part of a standard triple peel, and it happens when a ball is peeled through two wickets on a single turn. Although the double peel occurs on a single turn, it does not necessarily occur on successive strokes.

*The Triple Peel*  The triple peel is a move in which, as you go round with your ball, you peel your partner's ball through the last three hoops and peg both balls out. This ends the game. This is a difficult and exact series of shots, and a triple is something you rarely see, even in "A" competition.

*Delayed Triple Peel*  Sometimes the situation arises when you might temporarily abandon the triple peel and resume it during your next turn. This move is called a delayed triple peel.

*Quadruple Peel*  Peeling through four hoops is called a quadruple peel. It is usually seen only in doubles when assisting a weaker partner.

*Quintuple Peel*  A five wicket peel. It rarely occurs.

*Sextuple Peel*  This is part of a plan to finish the game in two turns, without giving your opponents a chance to hit. Several international championships have been won by using a sextuple.

*The Irish Peel*  This is a roll shot that sends both balls through the hoop with the same stroke. It should only be attempted when you are in front of and near the hoop.

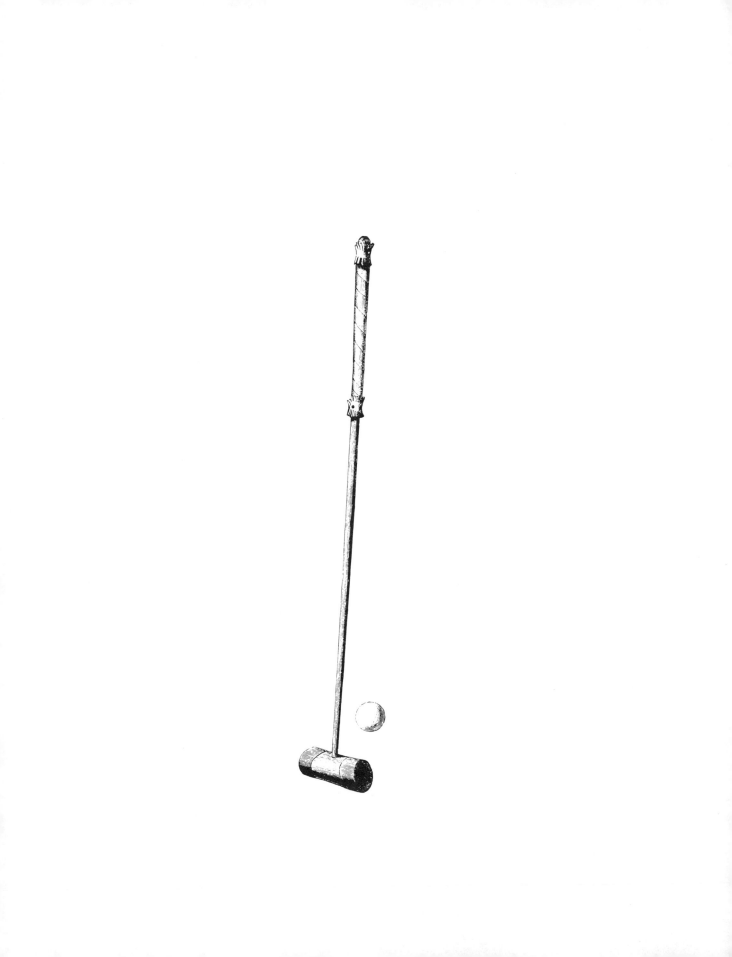

*One starts out pleasantly and laughingly enough; but before the third arch is reached, there may be a tightening of the lips, an abandonment of all decent impulses, with only the will to win firmly established in one's heart."*
*—Charles Hanson Towne,*
*Croquet-Social Shock Absorber,*
*Arts and Decoration, Aug. 1932*

# X
# *Openings*

As you remember, all balls enter the game a mallet's length from the first wicket, and all are dead until they run that wicket. This rule allows you to head right for the first hoop without fear of being roqueted or leaving your opponent with the possibility of a break. Thus jockeying for opening position is unnecessary, and strategy and positional play do not really enter the game until you run the first wicket. In the British game, however, all balls are live when the game begins, and a great deal of care is necessary in your approach to the first hoop. We are including a short briefing on British opening strategy as an introduction to some of the aspects of croquet tactics which will be covered more fully in a later chapter.

If an inexperienced player were watching the start of a championship croquet match in Britain, the chances are excellent that he would rapidly become confused. For instead of shooting for the first wicket, as under American rules, the British player seemingly ignores the first hoop and, instead, shoots his balls to the side boundaries or the corners. Once you become aware of the strategy and tactics involved, this seemingly irrational behavior begins to make perfect sense.

As you gain experience, it soon becomes obvious that it is vitally important to control or be able to use as many of the balls as possible, while preventing your opponent from doing so. Gaining control of the play by superior positioning is called "getting the innings." This means that you have managed to arrange your balls in such a way that you are more likely to score points in the near future than your opponent. When you are in this position you are said to be "in."

For this reason, since the fourth ball entering the game is the one that has the best chance for an immediate break, having the other three balls on the court to shoot at, the player playing under this rule begins his game by going for the boundaries or the corners. The odds against running the first wicket from the boundary line, where British play starts, are great. Since you are already alive, if you miss that shot, you leave yourself in a vulnerable position, where you can be hit by your opponent and, hence, lose the innings. So the experienced player tries to avoid putting his balls in the center of the court, always aware of what he is leaving his foe to shoot at.

With this in mind, a basic standard opening has evolved, one that is used in nine of ten British games. In our hypothetical game, player A plays the blue and black balls and goes first. Player B plays the red and yellow balls. In opening the game player A sends his first ball, say black, to a point on the east boundary near the fourth corner. Player B sends his first ball, red, to a point on the west boundary, usually seven to ten yards from the first corner. In playing this shot, player B hopes to entice his opponent into shooting for this ball with blue, and, he hopes, missing it. This is called "laying a tice." The length of the tice is important, as the shot must appear appetizing and yet not be too easy.

Player A now has two options for his next shot. He can decide not to accept the tice and shoot blue to black on the east boundary. In playing this shot, A hopes that player B will not now hit red with his yellow ball. Player A can also decide to accept the tice, aiming if he misses to go into the second corner. He does this to prevent his opponent from doing the same. If the shot is missed, A has lost the innings, but black and blue are now near opposite corners of the court, and, hence, of little use to player B. If A does hit red, he can then take croquet and knock red to a spot where B would be unlikely to be able to hit it, such as the peg. With his continuation shot he can then send blue to join black.

Player B now shoots at red, if A has not already roqueted it. He aims for the second corner if he misses, provided that A has not already gone there. In order to do this, he must play yellow from the first corner spot. If B makes the roquet on red he has got the innings, and he can now get to the business of running wickets and setting up his breaks. If B misses the shot, A would have the innings, as his balls are together on the east boundary for an easy roquet. If player A has missed the tice and gone into the second corner, player B can shoot at red, so that, if he misses, the ball will be replaced on the yard line near yellow. If blue hits this tice, he will have the innings, and it will be difficult to seize them.

As you can see, under these British rules the opening is an important part of the game. When learning these openings, as well

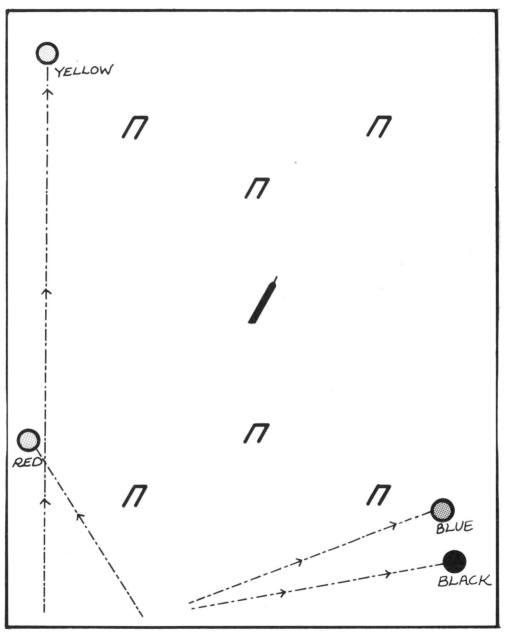

The standard British opening.

as breaks and strategy, which are covered elsewhere, it will be much clearer if you take the balls to the course and run through the opening shot by shot. The seemingly complicated maneuvering will then begin to make sense and become relatively easy to understand.

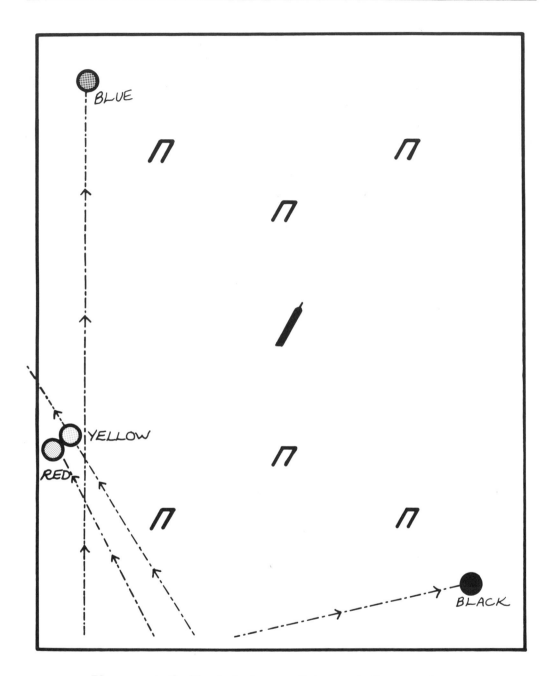

**Blue accepts the 'tice but misses and goes on to the second corner.**

Now that we have gotten the balls into the game, it is time to go on to
the general strategy of croquet.

78

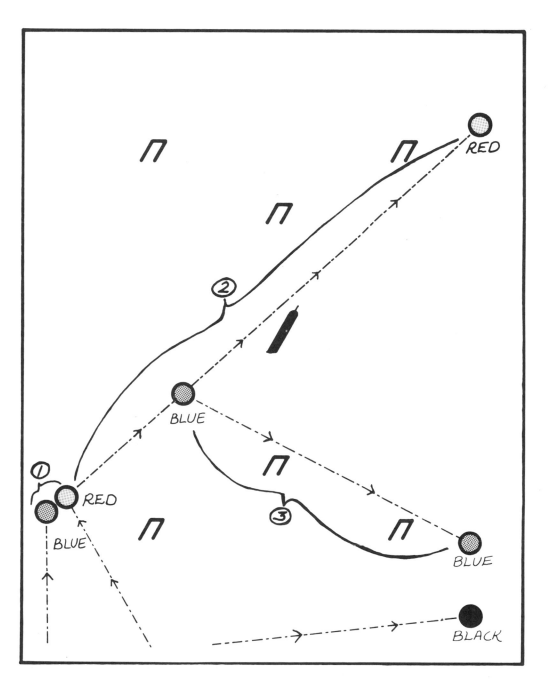

**Blue accepts the 'tice and makes it. Blue then moves red to corner 3 on the ensuing croquet shot, and then joins up with black on the continuation shot.**

*Its not the same game. Its an absolutely different game, that's the trouble. Its a different game and everyone thinks its a kids game or an old lady's game or some damn thing.*

—Zanuck

# XI
# Breaks

The good croquet player tries to place the balls in such a way that, by a combination of roquets, croquet shots, and continuation shots, he is able to make more than one hoop in his turn. Making more than one wicket in your turn is called making a break. This is a highly desirable croquet tactic. Good players are sometimes able to make all the wickets in one turn, which is called making an all round break. Breaks can be made with two, three, or four balls, but the more balls involved, the easier the break. We will discuss each type of break, and we suggest that you take the balls to the court and run through each of them, to get an idea of how they work, and to see them in action.

The two ball break is the simplest to follow but the most difficult to accomplish. Since there are only two balls involved, each shot has to be extremely accurate. One poor or off line shot will end your break. To see how the two ball break is accomplished, place two balls, say red and yellow, on the court, so that red is about two yards in *front* of the first hoop and yellow a foot behind red. You are playing yellow, and have a rush on red to the hoop. Gently rush red to the wicket so that it stops about two feet in front of the wicket and about six inches to one side. Since you have roqueted red, you now take croquet on that ball. Place yellow in contact with red so that they point to one side of the hoop, say left. With a stop shot, send yellow to about six inches in front of the hoop, with red stopping a few yards on the far side of the wicket. You can then run the wicket with yellow, making sure to hit it hard enough so that it stops just behind red. Now rush red to the second hoop. This entitles you to croquet on red. With your croquet shot, send yellow to in front of the second wicket, with red going past and to the right of that hoop. Run the second wicket with yellow, and you now have a rush on red to the third wicket. Using this same method, continue around the course. With only two balls in play, the slightest error will end your break, or at the very least, leave you with an extraordinarily difficult shot.

The pattern of sending a ball to the next wicket plus one is the basic pattern of all breaks, whether two, three, or four ball breaks. The ball that is sent to the next hoop plus one is called the pioneer ball.

The three ball break is easier to accomplish than the two ball break, since you have an extra ball to make use of, and, hence, more leeway in the accuracy of each shot. To run through the three ball break, place red and yellow as before, and add another ball, say blue, a few feet in front of the second wicket. Start the break as you did in the two ball break, approaching and running the first hoop. You now have three choices for your next shot. You can either roquet red gently, then send it with your croquet split shot to the third wicket, with yellow going to blue at the second hoop. This is a very difficult shot. You can also rush red half way to the second wicket, and attempt the split shot from this close range, or you can rush red directly to the third wicket. Take croquet from red, sending yellow to blue at the second hoop. Once you have done this, you can now roquet blue at the second wicket, approach and run it as in the two ball break. Then softly rush blue to the third hoop, and, with your croquet shot, send it to the fourth wicket so that yellow stops near red at the third hoop. If you have a perfect rush line on blue toward the fourth wicket, try to put it there on your rush shot. Then go to red at the third to make that hoop. Continue in the same fashion, sending red to the fifth wicket, and blue, after the fourth wicket, to the sixth wicket. Note the pattern of sending the ball to the next hoop plus one.

The four ball break is the easiest break to accomplish. Unlike the two or three ball breaks, the four ball break is made by making various detours around the course rather than heading right for the next wicket. Start the same as the three ball break, with black placed about three yards to the left of the stake. Run the first hoop as in the two and three ball breaks, and then roquet red gently to the third wicket. Now send yellow to black, trying to stay below black, but making sure to come within a yard or two of it. Roquet black gently and take off to blue, leaving black where it is. Now run the second wicket off blue, then roquet it gently. With your croquet shot, send blue to the fourth hoop, and yellow to black. Roquet black again, take off to red at the third wicket, leaving black near the stake, preferably a little to the right of it. Continue as before, sending the ball that you just ran the wicket with to the next hoop

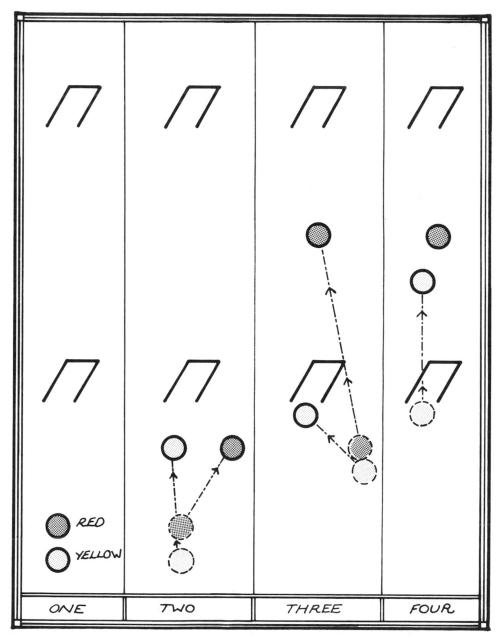

A 2-ball break. Yellow roquets red, then croquets red past the hoop, and then yellow runs the wicket himself.

plus one. This ball is the pioneer ball, and black, in this case, is known as the pivot ball. Then continue taking off from the pivot ball to the ball waiting at your next hoop.

This is the basic outline of the break. In the game, of course, you

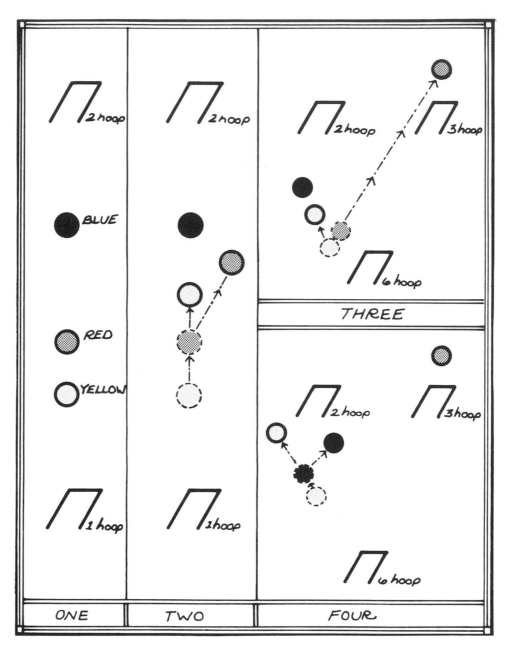

A 3-ball break. Yellow roquets red (2), then croquets red 2 hoops ahead (3),
leaving himself in a position to roquet blue. Yellow roquets blue (4), and then
moves to the next hoop, with the blue ball going to the far side of the wicket (5).

will have to maneuver the balls into position before you can make
the break, but with practice, you should be able to set up your own
breaks and take advantage of those that your opponent leaves for
you. Many Americans are not aware of the concept of making

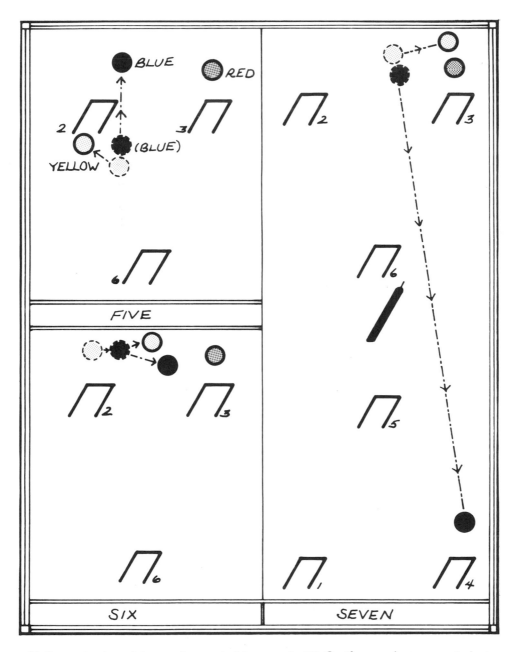

Yellow runs its wicket and roquets blue again (6). On the ensuing croquet shot (7), yellow hits blue to the fourth hoop, and leaves himself with a rush on red to the third hoop.

breaks, and, since few have practiced it, it is one of the most useful tools to learn for beginners eager to master opponents who may have played for years longer than they have.

*Do not imagine that the game is over when you give a sigh of relief because you are through the last hoop and have every reason to expect that you are about to peg out both balls. Do not relax your care by a hair breadth until both balls have been pegged out. There is no such thing as shots so easy that it never has been, and could not be, missed!"*
—Reverend G.F. Handel Elvey, 1910

# XII
# Pegging Out

Now we arrive at the decisive part of croquet known as the pegged-out or staked-out game. Once your ball has properly run through all its hoops, the next step for you is to peg it out, that is, to hit the final stake with your ball. If you peg both of your balls out, and do so before your opponent, you are the winner. During the staked-out game, a seemingly hopeless game can be won; likewise, a sudden defeat can be your fate. As in ordinary play, the usual basic strategic options are open to you in the pegging-out part of the game—you can shoot for the stake, play into a defensive position or bide your time until your foe shoots, hopefully misses, and places himself in a difficult position.

Don't relax and let up until both your balls are staked-out and you are the winner! Your final shots should be lined up with particular care, leaving yourself with easy rush shots to your last hoop(s). In doing this, remember not to leave yourself open as an easy target, and be especially careful not to provide your foe with a shot at both his proper hoop and at your ball. In keeping with this strategy, try to leave your opponent with only long and difficult shots.

Under certain conditions you may even find it advantageous to peg one of your opponent's balls out, and this is allowable under the rules. If you do peg out your opponent, you cut down the number of combinations he can use, and thus make it more difficult for him to keep or regain the innings. Staking-out an opponent's ball also gives you and your partner extra turns every other turn. It's a two-edged sword, of course, since *you* also lose the advantage of using the full complement of balls, and your own progress may be stalled. Remember, you can only peg-out a ball if it is a rover. In doubles, should you decide to remove an enemy ball from the game by staking it out, be sure that you peg out the better player. By so doing, you leave the fate of your opponents in the hands of the weaker foe.

Pegging an opponent out can also have the unnerving effect of disrupting your opponent's normal game, but unless you are skilled

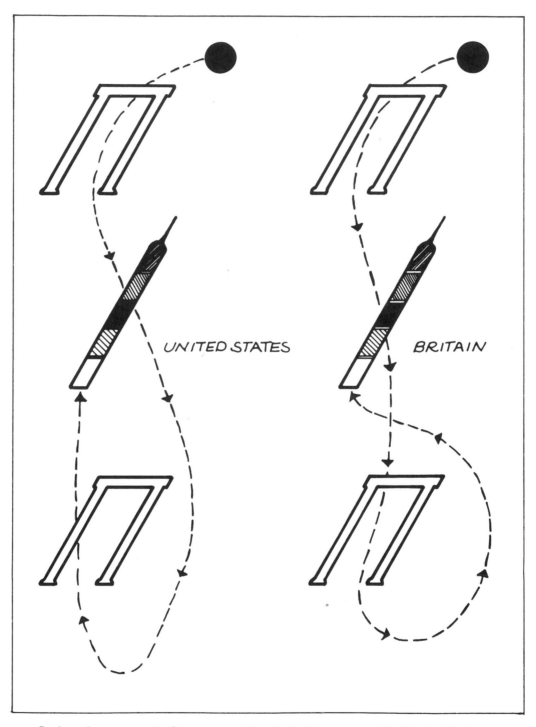

**In American croquet, always remember that when you run the final wicket you should be heading toward the stake.**

in the nuances of two- and three-ball play, it may unfortunately disturb your own style of play. Factors that will influence your decision to reduce the game to three or two balls are the comparative positions of your own and your opponent's backward ball, and your relative break-making abilities. You must also consider, when involved in a handicap game, the number of bisques which remain to yourself and your adversary.

There are many other items of strategy that you should be familiar with in order to be proficient in the two-ball game, or, games in which you or your foes have a one-ball advantage. First, consider the situation of having both balls in play, to your opponent's one. At this stage of the pegged-out game, you should try to pick up breaks whenever possible, minimizing, if you can, potential risks. In such a position, you might even try to go out on a three-ball break! Do not let your foe gain the innings, as this could have dire consequences so late in the game.

If you lack confidence in your break-making ability, try to advance just one or two hoops at a time. Try to wire your ball from your opponent whenever possible. This strategy, however, is difficult to accomplish if the lawn is uneven, as most are.

You may find that the best policy at this stage of the game is to shoot for a far boundary for defensive reasons, especially if you are unsure of your next move. This is the so-called "Thin Wire Principle," and using it sometimes entices your enemy into making a damaging move toward you, while you are in a position of relative safety.

If you have one rover, even if you are experienced and proficient in two ball play, never peg your ball out independently of your partner's ball; this avoids leaving your partner in a tenuous position. If you feel that you are suitably located for pegging both of your balls out, do not let such an opportunity pass. In any case, especially if your backward ball is ahead of the remaining enemy ball, try particularly hard to control the situation and dictate, if you are able, your foe's every move through shots of your own.

The strategy used in the situation of having one ball to your adversary's two is quite like that used in the reverse circumstances. It is, as always, crucial to prevent the enemy from undertaking a three-ball break. Be wary of going into a seemingly good position at the expense of giving your opponent a possible break. However, since it is essential for you to extend your turn for as long as you can, you must try to take advantage of all shooting opportunities. If you are shooting poorly, you can also hope to gain the innings through an enemy error. Try, if you can, to head off the enemy's lead ball.

Conversely, you can temporarily ignore your foe's position, and, instead, go for your own hoop or the stake. This might also impede your adversary's progress, as he might have to abandon his offensive game in an attempt to intercept your ball. Try, if you can, to make your final wickets on a single break, for a lapse here could prove fatal, with your foe so close to pegging-out. As in playing with a single ball advantage, with two balls you may fall back on the Thin-Wire Principle, hoping to lure the enemy into making a mistake. If you have a sizeable lead, you may decide to peg your foe's and one of your own balls out, thus beginning a two-ball game. Although some consider it questionable it goes without saying that you should not invite this situation unless your remaining ball is in a reasonable position to peg-out. Your weaponry is limited in two-ball play, but you should be able to finish out, either on a two-ball break or with single strokes.

You should consider two other factors before embarking on a two-ball game. First, do not fall so far behind that you can only rescue yourself through pure shooting. Secondly, when negotiating the difficult middle hoops, be sure not to leave yourself as a "sitting duck." When both players are going for the middle wickets, a situation similar to starting play develops, as the combatants try to creep into proper position, mutually avoiding the enemy. It often takes numerous shots to resolve this stage of the contest.

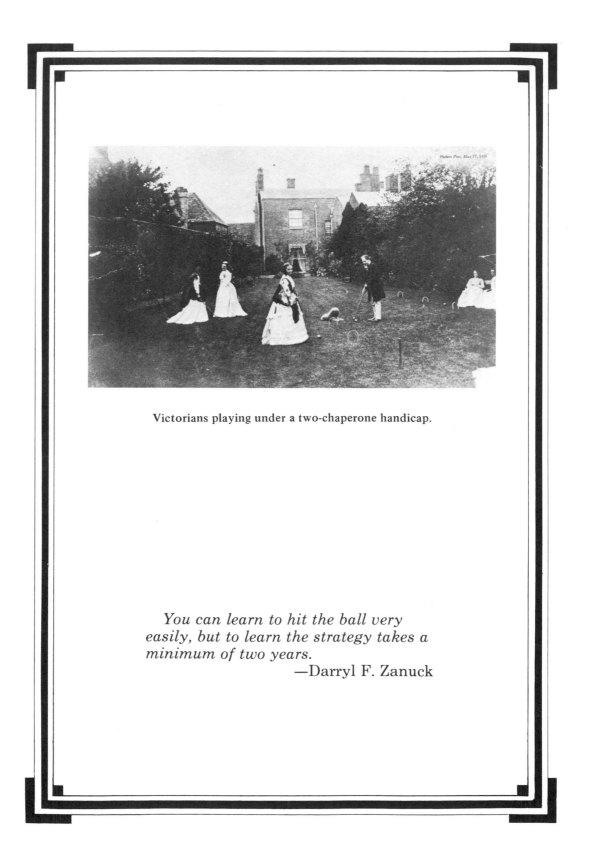

Victorians playing under a two-chaperone handicap.

*You can learn to hit the ball very easily, but to learn the strategy takes a minimum of two years.*
—Darryl F. Zanuck

# XIII
# Handicap Play

Croquet, like many sports, uses a system of handicapping to neutralize the differences in skill between players. The unit used in croquet, both in American and United Kingdom play, to express handicaps is called a bisque. The functions of bisques differ on each side of the Atlantic.

In American handicap tournaments, *all* players are assigned bisques, in a system usually ranging from the "scratch" player with none, to the beginner with as many as 20. Bisques in America are taken in the form of "do-over" shots. If you declare a bisque you are allowed to replace your ball at its point of origin and replay the shot last taken. You must use the ball last played, but you may attempt a different shot.

In both American and British croquet, the method used for allocating bisques is the same. That is, only the *inferior* of the players or teams is allowed to use the bisques. Let us say your handicap is 3 and your foe's is 5. In this match your opponent would receive 2 bisques.

In England, bisques are not "do-overs", but rather "free" turns, in the sense of extra shots taken at the conclusion of a stroke. The English handicap system also differs in that it presently ranges from $-5$ (currently given to only one player, Nigel Aspinall) to 16 for the novice. Before the present limits were set, Humphrey O. Hicks achieved the greatest handicap ever, with $-5\frac{1}{2}$.

Bisques generally play less of a role in American play than overseas, because American players are usually more evenly matched than their British cousins. Open handicap events in England frequently feature matches between players of widely disparate skill, and thus the English bisque can play more of a role in the outcome.

In England, a handicap unit called a *half-bisque* is used, along with bisques, in tourney competition. A half-bisque is similar to a bisque, but you cannot make a wicket on such a shot. It is generally used to improve position or to get out of harm's way. Some experts, including John W. Solomon, think that bisques in singles events should be, at the discretion of the player, split into half-bisques.

In U.S. tournaments, you are expected to use the handicap assigned to you prior to the start of play. If you do not have a handicap, it is the responsibility of the tournament manager to give one to you. If you are a beginner, you should receive a handicap from 16 to 20 (or, if playing under British rules, a handicap of at least 9) bisques. During play, the keeper of the deadness board is responsible for keeping track of the bisques.

## How to Use Your Bisques

When playing in a handicap game, there are certain facts about bisque use that you should keep in mind. You should save your bisques until you are approaching the end-game, or until you are in a crucial situation. Do not waste your bisques on simply any shot—try to bisque only when the situation justifies it. Don't bisque just to advance a single wicket, for the loss of a bisque outweighs the reward of one hoop.

Once you have reached the pegged-out game, use your bisques at the first opportunity. If you are three-ball dead, and are playing under American rules, you should also take a bisque to extricate yourself.

As in level play, it is generally to your advantage to open a handicap game after your opponent. In going last, you can use your bisques with all the balls in play, and thus potentially for your use. You wish to go last in the hope of making a break and seizing the innings before your opponent has a chance to use his or her bisques.

Always assess and re-evaluate the state of the game as your bisques, or those of your adversary, are exhausted. You might improve your game in handicap play, as bisques can give you a psychological edge. Bisques can also encourage you to attempt shots that you might ordinarily bypass. A good rule to remember is never to "go to bed with bisques." That is, never lose a game with unplayed bisques on your side.

One final tip—to improve your game, always try to play the "right shot." Don't look for the easy way out. You might, at first,

## BRITISH SCHEDULE OF BISQUES

| FULL GAME | 22 PTS. | 18 PTS. | 14 PTS. | FULL GAME | 22 PTS. | 18 PTS. | 14 PTS. |
|---|---|---|---|---|---|---|---|
| ½ | ½ | ½ | ½ | 10½ | 8½ | 7 | 5½ |
| 1 | 1 | ½ | ½ | 11 | 9½ | 7½ | 6 |
| 1½ | 1½ | 1 | 1 | 11½ | 9½ | 8 | 6 |
| 2 | 1½ | 1½ | 1 | 12 | 10 | 8½ | 6½ |
| 2½ | 2 | 1½ | 1½ | 12½ | 10½ | 8½ | 6½ |
| 3 | 2½ | 2 | 1½ | 13 | 11 | 9 | 7 |
| 3½ | 3 | 2½ | 2 | 13½ | 11½ | 9½ | 7½ |
| 4 | 3½ | 3 | 2 | 14 | 12 | 10 | 7½ |
| 4½ | 4 | 3 | 2 | 14½ | 12½ | 10 | 8 |
| 5 | 4 | 3½ | 2½ | 15 | 12½ | 10½ | 8 |
| 5½ | 4½ | 4 | 3 | 15½ | 13 | 10½ | 8½ |
| 6 | 5 | 4 | 3 | 16 | 13½ | 11 | 8½ |
| 6½ | 5½ | 4½ | 3½ | 16½ | 14 | 11½ | 9 |
| 7 | 6 | 5 | 4 | 17 | 14½ | 12 | 9½ |
| 7½ | 6½ | 5 | 4 | 17½ | 15 | 12 | 9½ |
| 8 | 7 | 5½ | 4½ | 18 | 15 | 12½ | 9½ |
| 8½ | 7 | 6 | 4½ | 18½ | 15½ | 13 | 10 |
| 9 | 7½ | 6 | 5 | 19 | 16 | 13 | 10 |
| 9½ | 8 | 6½ | 5 | 19½ | 16½ | 13½ | 10½ |
| 10 | 8½ | 7 | 5½ | | | | |

English bisque schedule. There is no standard American counterpart.

sacrifice some wins because of daring play, but if you extend your skills, have patience and practice your game, immense satisfaction will soon be yours. You may even lower your handicap!

## Handicap Doubles

Generally speaking, bisque-taking in handicap doubles is similar to singles play. In the United Kingdom, team handicaps are added together, and half the difference between the two is the number of bisques that the weaker side receives. In America, the same is true, but only the weaker player on the side receives the bisque. In doubles, stronger players should make the tactical decisions that are in doubt, and they should gently guide the moves of the inferior partner. The best player can either stay behind to aid his partner, and then finish out with a double or triple peel when they are close to staking-out, or he can simply mirror the moves of the weaker partner and finish the course hoop to hoop.

You do not want to stray too far from your partner, in order to avoid leaving either of you in a vulnerable position. You also want your partner to be located where he can help your own progress around the course. An English rule restriction is that in some doubles handicap events you cannot peel your partner through more than four hoops. This is designed to prevent doubles matches from becoming "specialized singles," with the inferior player having little or no effect on the game.

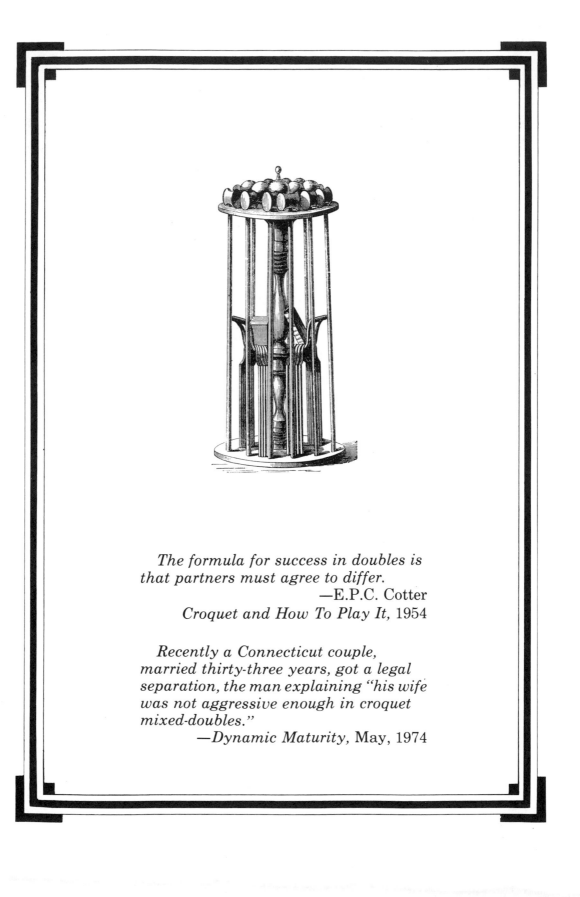

*The formula for success in doubles is
that partners must agree to differ.*
—E.P.C. Cotter
*Croquet and How To Play It,* 1954

*Recently a Connecticut couple,
married thirty-three years, got a legal
separation, the man explaining "his wife
was not aggressive enough in croquet
mixed-doubles."*
—*Dynamic Maturity,* May, 1974

# XIV
# Doubles

Even though croquet is designed to be played by two or four players, the doubles variety is considered to have some critical flaws. Chief among them is that the level of play in doubles can fall far below the individual abilities of the four players. Unless you and your partner are relatively closely matched and used to competing together, you will find that you may stray from your normal playing pattern in attempting to compensate for an inferior partner. This can downgrade the quality of play and spectator appeal alike.

Another complaint is that A-level players are frequently paired with novices, to prevent certain tandems from running away from the field. In American tournament play, however, players are generally paired more evenly than in English tournaments, so that in the States, at least, this criticism is not applicable.

Doubles croquet has essentially the same rules as those set forth for singles play. As a team, you are permitted to consult to a limited degree, but most consultation of this sort should be kept to a bare minimum—unless you are a "coarse and ill-refined" player. You are not allowed to receive advice from anyone but your partner.

As the rules for singles and doubles are similar, so too is the strategy involved, especially if all the players are fairly evenly matched. Differences do appear in tactics when the participants are mismatched, so it is crucial to keep in mind the relative abilities of your foes, as well as the skills of you and your partner.

If your side is evenly matched, try to stick to your normal approaches to the game. Decide, as a team, how the ball is to be played, and then let the striker play the ball as well as he or she can. Try to keep your inferior opponent's ball as the backward ball, with the stronger foe progressing at a faster pace so as to be susceptible to being staked-out. Needless to say, avoid leaving possible breaks, even for an inept opponent.

If you have a weaker partner, endeavor to help him or her to progress several wickets ahead of your own ball. Don't try to move too far with your ball while you are aiding your partner, as you may become vulnerable to being pegged-out.

In spite of the critical comments aimed at the doubles form of croquet, doubles can be exhilarating, both to play and watch. This is especially true of the major, A-flight doubles events.

*courtesy of PGA National, Home of the United States Croquet Association*

**A promising partnership.**

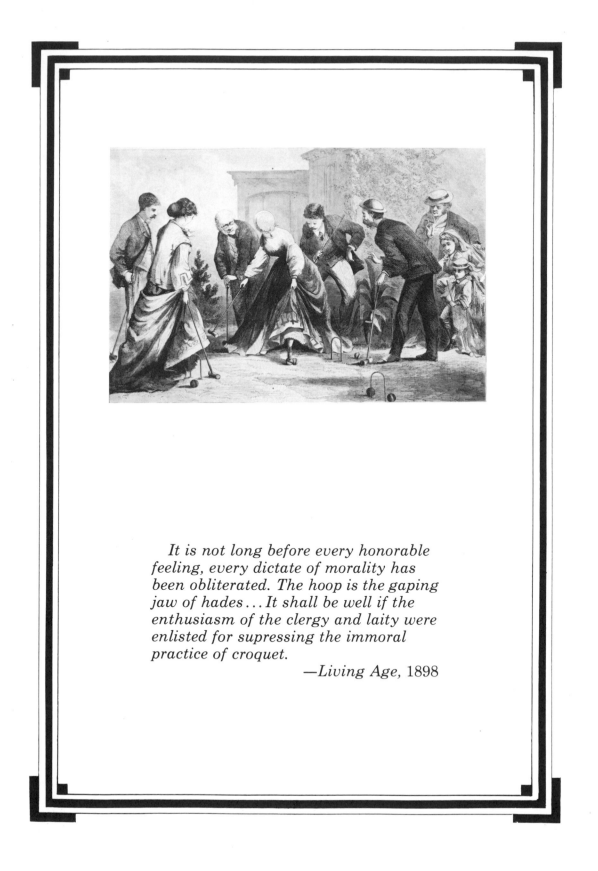

*It is not long before every honorable feeling, every dictate of morality has been obliterated. The hoop is the gaping jaw of hades . . . It shall be well if the enthusiasm of the clergy and laity were enlisted for supressing the immoral practice of croquet.*

*—Living Age, 1898*

# XV
# Etiquette, Dress and Dirty Play

There is perhaps no other game with rules so precise as croquet. For this reason, croquet etiquette is almost a redundancy: the by-laws—British or American—proscribe all but the most unseemly behavior, and the assignment of referees provides for settlements of disputes which, if not entirely amicable, at least allow the actual playing to continue.

The following, while not including specific rules or penalty-related action, should be considered important and helpful to the conduct and enjoyment of the game.

A player should not remain on the court in line of sight or area of visibility while his adversary is playing or move onto it until it is clear that he is finished or may be about to take a questionable stroke. A player should play his strokes as quickly as possible, and in doubles should avoid wasting time in prolonged discussion with his partner (more than 60 seconds is considered excessive).

Spectators should abstain from audible comments on the game, from offering advice to players during a game; and from calling attention to any error committed or about to be committed by any player. A spectator may reply to a question by a player on a point of fact with the consent of the adversary. A player should not take advantage of any error or omission unnoticed by himself or his partner to which his attention has been drawn during the game by the comments or attitudes of spectators.

No player is entitled to advice from anyone other than his partner in doubles. It must be a matter of conscience how a player acts when in receipt of unsolicited information or advice. Warning a player other than a partner that he is about to run a wrong wicket or play with the wrong ball constitutes advice and in tournaments players and spectators are not allowed to do this.

No mark shall be made, either inside or outside the court, for the purpose of guiding the striker in the direction or strength of a stroke. A partner may use his mallet to indicate a spot, but it must be recovered before the stroke.

A player about to play a stroke, of which either the fairness or the effect (i.e. possible foul or when aiming at a ball near a wicket) may be doubtful, should suggest that a referee be called to watch the stroke. If a ball has to be replaced because of the carelessness of a player, the offending party should ordinarily defer to the opinion of the other. When the question is whether a roquet has been made on a ball or whether a ball has moved, the gentlemanly or positive opinion is generally to be preferred to the negative opinion. If there are any reliable witnesses the players should agree to consult them in order to solve differences; but no player should consult a witness without the express permission of the other player.

The striker should not test whether a ball has run a wicket by placing his mallet against the wicket without first consulting his opponent. Any such test should be made in conjunction with the opponent or if either party desires, by a referee or independent person. The same principle applies when the question is whether a ball is out of bounds, or whether it may be lifted, moved or wiped if the position of replacement is critical. All such decisions made between strokes should be made jointly.

In tournaments, a referee should always be called before a questionable stroke, and all disputes should be referred to a referee. If the opponent fails to call a referee *before* a questionable stroke, he may not afterwards appeal the decision. If the adversary believes that the striker is making faults such as "pushing" or "double tapping", he should inform the striker to have a referee called to watch the stroke.

The remarks in this section are directed to the coarse player, the man who works literally within the rules, but who is morally depraved. The following are some of his tactics.

*The Psyche Out.* Prior to a match, he will approach an opponent humbly and apologetically, tugging his forelock and bemoaning his own dismal health, or hangover, and inept playing style. This performance must be done deftly and with maximum sincerity, for a too-broad technique will simply not work. The opponent is to be brought only to the point of thinking he is indeed wasting his time with this amateur and of feeling sorry for him. This skillfully-induced feeling of pity and annoyance can lead to complacent play on the opponent's part. The coarse player will continue to apologize, proclaiming his great luck in making his shots, good or bad. The charade continues through the eighth wicket, at which point . . .

*The Stall* is used. This is to be employed judiciously. No shot is played until all possibilities are utterly exhausted. The proper coarse technique is to worry every potential lie (aloud), decide on a wrong shot, discover the better way, keeping up a low-pitched, nearly inaudible monologue the entire time. This monologue is crucial to the coarse player; it is masked as "thinking aloud" and if the aggrieved opponent is finally stung into saying, "For God's sake, man—shoot," an immediate reversion to the earlier humility is employed, now coupled with the hurt expression of the inferior player who is not being given a chance to play a decent game against a ferocious opponent. The coarse player will immediately ask the referee if any breach of time has taken place; the tone of voice will suggest harassment and persecution.

He will, of course, start reminding his opponent of *his* passing time immediately after time has been called. If an opponent is allowed 45 seconds to stalk or plan the next shot, the coarse player will start displaying his impatience after 20 seconds or so. Naturally, this is not done with any petulance, but with the righteousness of his avowed belief that the 60 seconds has expired.

By now the opponent of the coarse player may be angry enough to misplay. Under no circumstances will he be advised prior to making his shot. However, should he play on a dead ball, he will be so informed after the shot, in a helpful, solicitious voice, tinged with true regret.

The throwing of the mallet should always be up in the air. It should never be directed at an opponent, referee or onlooker.

The coarse player will usually appear late for a match and will never apologize for his tardiness. He may even inquire as to why people are standing around. Should he arrive before his opponent, he will, of course, either accuse his opponent of deliberately holding up beginning play by addressing loud remarks to the gallery about the virtues of punctuality, the essential bad manners of later comers, etc. The remarks will never be directed to the opponent, but should be made in his hearing.

If this tactic is too aggressive or the opponent has a volatile temperament (see reference to mallet throwing), sly suggestions as to fear causing lateness can be brought into play.

105

Since croquet garb is generally informal, the coarse player might appear in a business suit or dinner clothes, wearing them with the air of one who has more important things to do.

When the opponent is stalking his ball, the coarse player will try to make a distracting sound of maximum irritation. Popping gum, cracking knuckles, sucking teeth and whistling are all examples of noises which have turned coarse players into champions. Concurrent with the noise ploy, remarks to the gallery regarding the extraordinary improvement X is showing in his game and his great luck should also be made. The suggestion that he is playing above his head today is the most effective, as is half-hearted applause after an adequate but not difficult shot. Applause is never to be used when a truly fine shot is made—the coarse player did not see it. The suggestion—only suggestion—is that there is some trickery involved.

In the opening wickets, the coarse player will use destroy shots and approaches as often as possible.

Coarse players are a fact of croquet life, and while it is natural to deplore this playing style, the new player should be aware of this streak of ferocity in order to guard against it.

# DRESS

The proper croquet garb, like the game itself, is determined by quiet good taste. Only all-white clothes can be worn in USCA sanctioned tournaments, but essentially the rules for dress are flexible, limited only by practical rules of comfort. The game is a demanding one and calls for a comfortable uniform. Freedom of motion is the ultimate criterion.

## Shoes

Out of consideration for the course, the croquet shoe should be soft and flat soled. The soft rule is a good one; not only is the course protected but the player is guaranteed maximum foot comfort for the grueling hours ahead. Whether the shoe is a Gucci slip-on, a Topsider, Adidas sneakers or disreputable jogging shoes is determined by the breeding and personal preference of the individual. Champion players have been known to favor all varieties, with a

surprising number opting for the disreputable, albeit well broken-in, tennis shoe. Indeed, some in the U.S. have played barefoot. Style must be sacrificed only insofar as protection of the playing surface is concerned. Shoes with sharp heels are not to be worn under any circumstances during play.

## The Shirt

Skillful players at any level will take every advantage to improve their game. Many croquet buffs believe the generously cut shirt provides a more fluid swing and so recommend wearing a shirt a size larger than normally worn. Opponents of the bigger-shirt theory hold that the extra material may in fact impede the swing by increasing wind resistance; logically, they extend their thinking by wearing snug, wrinkle-free pullover short-sleeved shirts, preferably of a synthetic material. The synthetic fabric, according to these theorists, will not absorb moisture and will therefore be of lighter weight during the course of the play. Too, they feel the synthetic fabric will move more freely through the air.

It's an argument that has gone on for some time, and the rule book for croquet sensibly ignores it. A shirt or top (particularly for women players) should be worn; the style and fabric to be chosen and determined by one's own standards of playing comfort.

English traditionalists ask that the croquet shirt remain a white broadcloth Sea Island pima cotton, the long sleeves rolled to just below the elbow.

## The Trousers or Skirt

White flannel is still worn by serious players in England, and it is hard to fault the elegance of this classic garb. However, in croquet, alas like in too many things, standards have changed over the years and skirts and trousers of every conceivable cut and fabric are now seen on the croquet court. Croquet players, like all athletes, have their superstitions. In consequence, the "lucky" blue-jeans, flannels or shorts will be worn repeatedly. There are known instances of players being requested to change their luck and their trousers, but again, the rules are wisely flexible in this regard. The selection of color, fabric and cut of skirt or trousers remains the exclusive province of the wearer.

## Head Gear

Fortunately for civilized play, the protective helmet is no longer needed. At one point in croquet's checkered history, the mallet was used as imaginatively as today's hockey stick, a flexibility that encouraged the wearing of leather caps not too dissimilar from the football helmet. Happily or not, these are bygone days.

The billed cap is to be worn only for protection against the heat and glare of the sun. An attempt at a team uniform—to include the visored cap emblazoned with team colors—simply did not catch on. Frankly, caps are considered effete by seasoned players, and are openly discouraged except when playing in the tropics or Australia.

### Socks

White, of cotton or wool, is the preferred color sock. The sock should reach well above the ankle, but need not reach mid-calf. Croquet is nothing if not a realistic game. Many players do not wear socks at all.

### Foul Weather Croquet Gear

One of the hardier games, croquet provides for continued play even in the face of inclemency. Since a game will not be delayed until puddles begin to form on the court, players are advised to make provision for playing in the rain.

The standards for rainwear are simple: usually a large umbrella held over the head of the player by his partner. Boots and raincoats are generally not worn since they act as obvious impediments to a clean swing. There are no specifications regarding the size or color of the umbrella, but a player is under no obligation to share or to offer to share an umbrella with an opponent foolish enough not to provide for the vagaries of the weather.

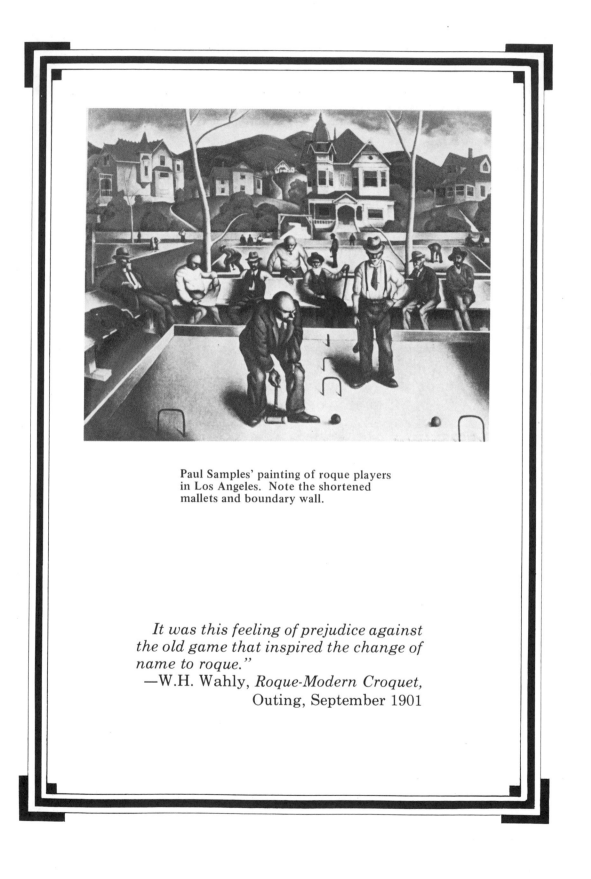

Paul Samples' painting of roque players
in Los Angeles. Note the shortened
mallets and boundary wall.

*It was this feeling of prejudice against
the old game that inspired the change of
name to roque."*
—W.H. Wahly, *Roque-Modern Croquet,*
Outing, September 1901

# XVI
# Roque

A first cousin of croquet is roque, a North American game incorporating elements of both croquet and billiards. The American Roque League has clubs from coast to coast and has quietly and uninterruptedly been holding tournaments and crowning champions since the 1880's. Once known as the National Croquet Association, the "C" and the "t" were dropped in 1899 to differentiate between the two sports, and thus, we now have "roque."

Roque is billed immodestly as the "game of the century" and, while it may have gone virtually unnoticed by the general public, it did surface long enough to be included as an Olympic sport in 1904. Not surprisingly, an American named Charles Jacobus took the gold medal, and since roque was dropped as soon as the Olympics left St. Louis, it is one of those rare Olympic events that has never been won by a non-American.

While there are many differences between roque and croquet, the most noticeable one is that a roque court is bounded on all sides by a twelve inch high cement wall. This wall, slightly cut in at the base, is used for bank shots much like the cushions of a billiard table, and allows for variations which are impossible on a croquet court. The roque court is sixty by thirty feet, as compared to croquet's course of one hundred and five by eighty-four feet, and is sanded rather than grassy. The wickets are steel and the area between the wickets is 3-3/8 inches wide, about the same as in croquet. The balls are hard rubber and are an eighth of an inch smaller than the wicket clearance, making roque as demanding as croquet when it comes to accuracy.

The mallets used in the two sports are also different. The roque mallet has a short shaft and is usually played with one hand. One end of the mallet head is hard—usually metal—and even ivory has been used. The other end is soft rubber. Although some players use one or the other end exclusively, the rubber end is usually better for short shots and the hard end for longer hits.

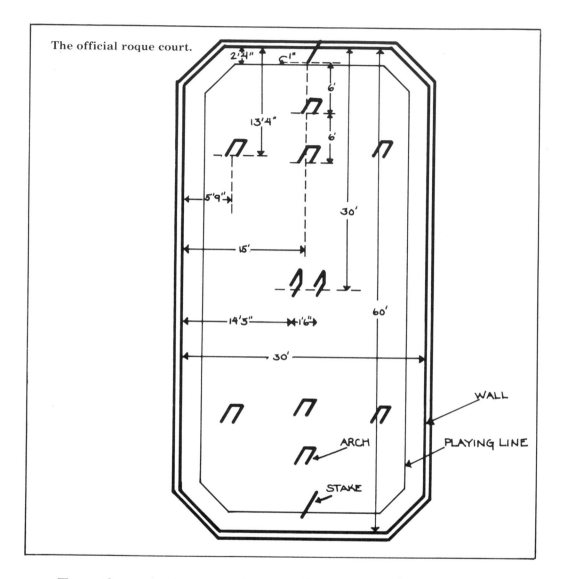

The official roque court.

Two, three or four people can play a roque game, but if three play, two players get one ball each and the third uses two balls. As with billiards, the starting sequence is determined by lagging balls toward the playing line. The order of red, yellow, blue and black is followed, but unlike croquet, the game is started by placing each of the balls at the four boundary-line corners of the court. When the game begins all balls are live on each other—unlike most American croquet variations—and, as it is virtually impossible to make a hoop on the opening shot, there are many bank shots used at the beginning of a roque game to jockey for position.

The emblem of the American Roque League, showing roque mallets and roque wicket.

The object of roque is to score thirty-two points—sixteen on each ball—or the most points in the allotted time. If all sixteen points are scored on a single turn it is called a "homerun" and, since roque scores are kept by innings, the game would be over in the first inning. There are usually ten innings in a game, although tournaments often take fifteen.

Roque wickets are run differently from those in croquet. The side hoops can only be made by using the "hot ball" (the ball to be played next by your opponent) or as a solo shot, without assistance. This rule greatly reduces the chances of a homerun. The center arches are played as if they are a single arch, or they can be made in successive turns, as long as the ball stays between the hoops and does not hit a live ball. As you can see, the use of a break is especially necessary around the center.

After a ball makes all its points except the stake, it becomes a rover, as in croquet. When both partners have become rovers, the striker must complete the game by roqueting his partner's ball against the stake, and then hitting the stake with his own ball on the next shot. Incidentally, the jump shot is not legal in roque.

These are the simple outlines of a very complicated game, and it is not our intent to cover all the rules and differences between roque and croquet in one chapter. The American Roque League, now in Dallas, will provide a list of clubs, rules, a book of strategy, and even diagrams on how to construct a roque court. The best advice is to contact them before you start cementing in your back yard.

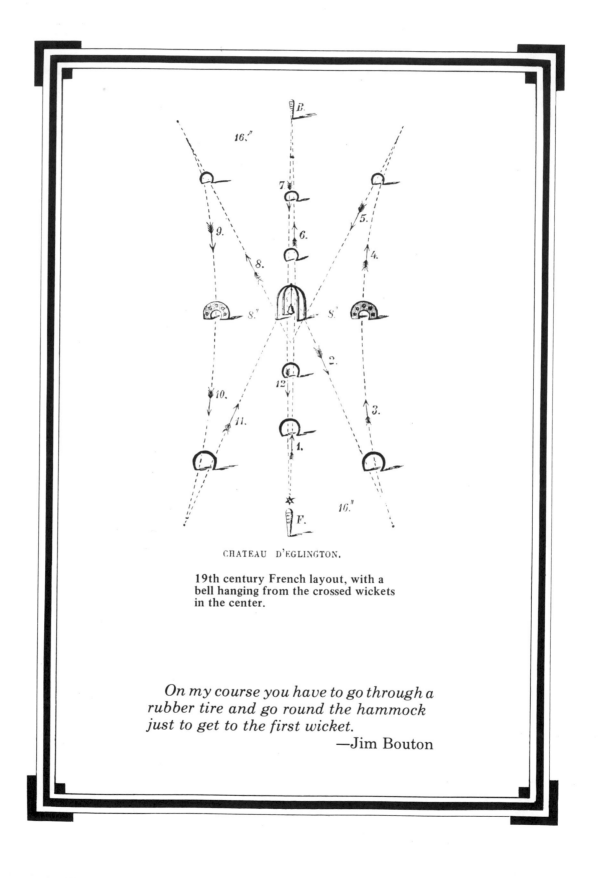

CHATEAU D'EGLINGTON.

19th century French layout, with a
bell hanging from the crossed wickets
in the center.

*On my course you have to go through a
rubber tire and go round the hammock
just to get to the first wicket.*
— Jim Bouton

# XVII
# *Variations*

Although the primary concern of our book is the official six-hoop game of croquet, there are, of course, numerous variations of the standard game. Some are played under the auspices of official bodies, while others are strictly on the level of "pick-up" games. In any case, no treatment of croquet would be complete without a look at the off-shoots of the parent game.

The SHORTENED GAME, either played over a course of fewer hoops, or abbreviated by a time-limit, is hardly a variation at all, in that it is essentially the same as the usual version. Although most players dislike shorter games, there are occasions when they must be used, sometimes even in serious tournament play. An over-sized entry frequently determines the use of limitations, although some tournaments only limit the participants (and raise the entry fees) to avoid shortening events. As we will discuss later, there are also instances when the lack of available space necessitates a smaller course, and thus, a shorter game. In defense of this variety of croquet it should be pointed out that it can be kinder to the spectator to watch a shortened game than for him to view inept players working interminably to end the game.

For the shortened game, the standard twenty-six point course can be altered in several ways. For a contest of TWENTY-TWO points, play starts with all players going for the third hoop. If a game is further reduced to EIGHTEEN points, play begins either with all clips on hoop five, or with all balls being for the first hoop. In the latter case, the peg-point is attempted after two-back, thus omitting hoops three-back through rover. Another method of setting up an eighteen-point game is to have the players begin with one ball for hoop one and the other for three-back.

An even shorter variety of croquet is the FOURTEEN-point game. Here the balls are put into play as if it were a regulation-length game, but you peg out after scoring the sixth hoop.

Once the course layout is settled upon, all shortened games are played under the accepted rules, with a few exceptions. There is a limit placed on the number of hoops through which you can peel your partner. Secondly, in short handicap games, the number of bisques assigned to you will be reduced in proportion to the length of the game.

In games shortened by a time-limit, play proceeds as usual, but is suspended after an arbitrary, but previously arranged time. Each player is allowed to complete his turn once the time-limit is reached.

Let us now look at croquet when it is played under the standard rules, but on a MODIFIED COURSE. In such games, the course is reduced in size to fit the existing land space. All markings and boundaries are scaled down accordingly. In extremely cramped surroundings, you should use the largest available rectangular plot of land. On such small courts, it may also be advisable to reduce the game to twenty-two points. Aside from the altered dimensions, these games are played under normal rules.

Although one naturally assumes that croquet is only a game for the outdoors, there is an officially-played INDOOR version. Since the early Sixties, in fact, croquet has been played inside under the auspices of England's stately Roehampton Club.

Indoor croquet is played on a carpet, generally no more than ten yards by eight yards in size (although there are no strictly standardized dimensions). The balls are the same as those used in snooker (small and with a very smooth surface), and only three are used. One is red, one blue and the third, considered neutral, is painted white. Only three are used for a good reason—break-making would simply be too easy in this game if the usual four balls were used.

Mallets are scaled down, but not in length. The hoops and pegs are forged from steel, and are attached by nails to floorboards under the playing carpet. Otherwise, the proportions and settings for this variety are the same as those for the outdoor game.

POLO, or ROBBER CROQUET, is a short, but entertaining variety of croquet. Play starts with all balls introduced into the game from the South boundary (A-baulk line). You must run the first hoop before you are capable of scoring and making roquets. Running a hoop, hitting the peg, or making a roquet will earn you an extra stroke. Running the first hoop is worth a single point, thereafter all hoops are worth two points.

You are not allowed to shoot for the same hoop or peg on two consecutive turns. When you make a roquet off an enemy ball, that ball becomes dead. The dead ball must then be re-introduced from the South boundary, and, again, run hoop one before it can score further points.

Here enters the "robber" aspect of the game, for a roquet off an opponent's ball also allows you to steal all enemy points below ten, and add them to your own total. Once you or your opponent scores ten points, those, and all subsequent groups of ten are immune from theft. Forty points wins a game of robber croquet.

A 19th century indoor course in Elyria, Ohio.

One of the more bizarre varieties of croquet is the game called OFFICIAL REGULATION CROQUET. Played under the jurisdiction of the American Roque League, this game features a smooth, hard-surface court of forty by seventy-five feet, with boundaries formed by a low concrete wall. An official roque court is sometimes used for official regulation croquet as well.

This type of croquet uses a setting of ten steel hoops. These are 3-3/4 inches wide, and are nine inches above the ground. The balls are made of hard rubber, are 3-3/8 inches in diameter, and have a standard weight of twelve ounces. Official roque mallets are used.

On the relatively small course, the two center hoops are placed eighteen inches apart, and at right angles to the other wickets. The side or corner wickets are placed so that they face in the direction of the center hoops (at a 45° angle). The others face in the normal direction. The concrete wall can be used for making carom shots, a stroke peculiar to roque and this type of croquet. The wall can thus provide you with a legitimate shot, even though you appear to be unable to make a direct hit on the desired ball. The object of Official regulation croquet is to make as many hoops as possible before you relinquish your turn to your adversary.

KENTUCKY CROQUET was devised in the 1930's by a group of Louisville players, and is a blend of croquet and roque. Kentucky State Croquet Championships were first held in 1936. Soon after, the Kentucky Croquet Association was formed, and it remains the oldest continuously operating state croquet association in the United States.

A fast-paced court of clay lightly sprinkled with sand is used for Kentucky Croquet. Two stakes are placed at either end of the court, and ten wickets (two of them crossed in the center to make a "basket") are set up between these stakes. The balls are slightly smaller (3½ inches in diameter), colored red, white, blue and black, and are played in that order. The mallets are short-handled (18 inches) compared with the usual croquet mallet (36 inches).

If you wish to learn more about this variation, you can contact the Croquet Association of Kentucky in Louisville for a rules pamphlet. Kentucky Croquet was introduced into the Bluegrass State Games in 1987.

GOLF CROQUET, also known as CROQUET GOLF, is another interesting variation that is governed by standardized English and USCA rules. This game is croquet with the hoops treated as if they were holes on a golf course. All balls are always for the same hoop, and the first to run a particular one wins the "hole," with all the players then proceeding to the next hoop. Balls are played in a sequence of blue, red, black and yellow, and basically, the laws relating to ordinary play apply to golf croquet, with some exceptions.

When compared with "real" croquet, golf croquet is lacking in both strategy and variety of shots. It is, however, simple and easy to learn and gives excellent practice in some basic croquet fundamentals. Often this variation is used to introduce croquet to large groups of beginners. Golf croquet is perfect as a lawn party activity or a fund-raising event.

We have included USCA-approved rules for golf croquet in the

**Lawn pool, one of the myriad variations of croquet.**

rules section of this book.

GARDEN CROQUET is a variety that many undoubtedly regard as the true game of croquet. There is no uniformity in the rules for garden croquet, and regulations are frequently adjusted to conform to local conditions and whims. Garden croquet embodies many of the assets of the usual game, but it is neither as demanding nor as complex.

The manner in which the home course is set out is determined, obviously, by the existing space. The norm is to have as level a course as possible, but hills and natural obstacles can add spice to a home game. The size of your course is arbitrary, but many home croqueteers claim that fifty by one hundred feet are ideal dimensions. Perhaps you might also want to have areas of varying difficulty on your course.

119

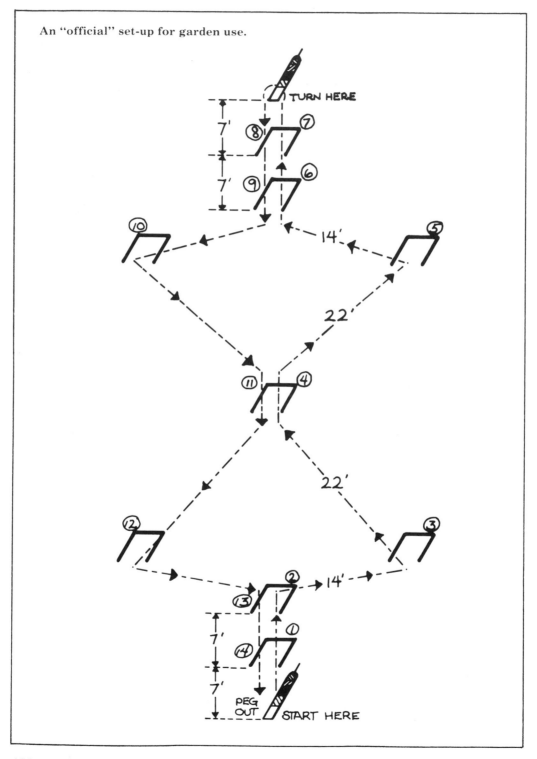

An "official" set-up for garden use.

Nine hoops and two wooden pegs are used in this variety of croquet. The boundary lines should be set roughly seven feet from the end wickets and five feet away from the side hoops. The wickets are generally made out of wire or steel rods.

Given the erratic nature of garden regulations, unorthodox wicket arrangements are permissible. You may devise spread wickets (a greater than usual distance apart), set two hoops in a crossed position (called a "pigpen"), or you can place the hoops in a circle. You can even do away with the boundaries if you wish.

Balls made from wood or hard rubber should be used in this type of play. The mallets can be rubber-headed or have wooden heads. The object of garden croquet is the same as for regulation play: to make as many hoops as possible during your turn.

Basically, the rules of ordinary play are to be observed in garden croquet, but a free interpretation of the rules is permissible (and usually inevitable), making this variety an interesting and unpredictable game. Purists may pooh-pooh it, but the home version remains a widely played, heartily enjoyed form of croquet.

*Note:* Forster Manufacturing Company, Inc., of Wilton, Maine, now includes official croquet rules in each of their Skowheegan croquet sets. Compiled and copyrighted by the United States Croquet Association, these are the first USCA-approved rules ever to grace a "backyard" croquet set. Millions of Americans, while still enjoying the 9-wicket "game" of croquet, will now have an opportunity to be enriched by the 6-wicket sport.

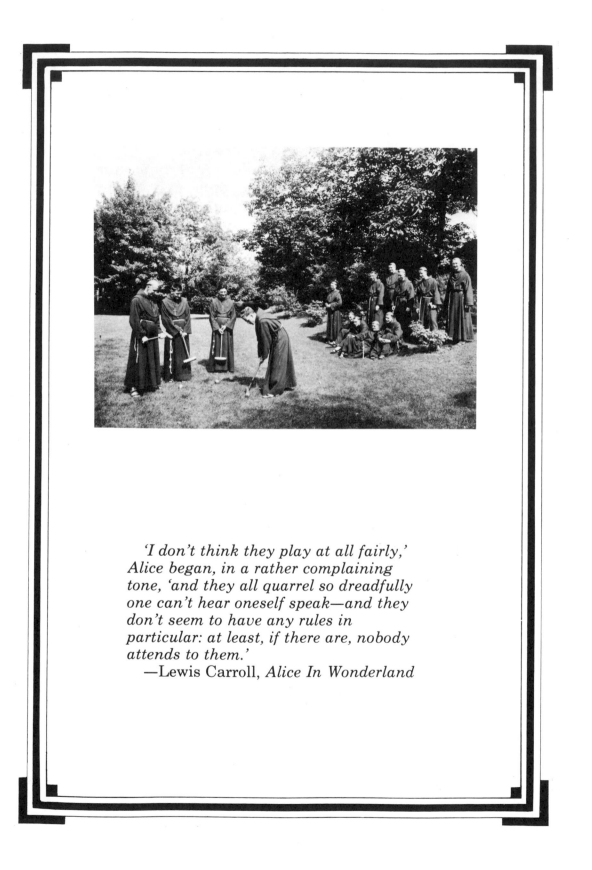

'I don't think they play at all fairly,'
Alice began, in a rather complaining
tone, 'and they all quarrel so dreadfully
one can't hear oneself speak—and they
don't seem to have any rules in
particular: at least, if there are, nobody
attends to them.'
—Lewis Carroll, *Alice In Wonderland*

# XVIII
# Rules

*THE NEW WAY TO PLAY CROQUET*
*APPROVED BY*
*THE UNITED STATES CROQUET ASSOCIATION*

*The following rules were compiled by the USCA and are copyrighted by them. They are now being placed in every Skowheegan croquet set made by the Forster Manufacturing Company, Inc., of Wilton, Maine. CROQUET is the first book published anywhere to include these rules. You might find it helpful, especially if you are a beginning player, to bring the balls to the court and walk through a game, experimenting with the various shots and testing different strategies outlined here and throughout the rest of the book.*

## INTRODUCTION TO THE
## GAME AND SPORT OF CROQUET

Before examining the basic objectives of the game, it would be helpful to learn and understand the language of croquet.

Four of the most important and frequently referred to terms are ROQUET, CROQUET, ALIVE and DEAD.

In the following section these and other key words are capitalized and if they are not made clear in the text, or in the rules, please refer to the Glossary.

### OBJECT OF THE GAME

The object of the game is to race your opponent(s) around a course of wickets and hit the finishing stake before he does (they do). The game can be played by either two people (*Individuals* or *Singles*), four (*Doubles*) or six people (*Triples*).

In the *Individual* game each player plays one ball and races his opponent to the finishing stake.

In the *Singles* game, each player plays two balls (either Blue

123

and Black or Red and Yellow), and attempts to score all the wicket points and finishing stake point for both of his balls before his adversary.

In *Doubles,* the game is played between two sides, each side consisting of two players. One team plays the Blue and Black balls and the other the Red and Yellow balls. Each player plays the same balls throughout the game. As in singles, the object is for one team to score the total possible points before their opponents.

In *Triples* the two sides consist of three players each with one team playing Blue, Black and Orange and the other Red, Yellow and Green.

In all games a ball scores a wicket point by passing through the wicket in the order and direction shown in the diagrams. This is known as RUNNING A WICKET. But a ball that has first hit another ball (roqueted) cannot thereafter in the same stroke bounce off and score a point for itself. A ball that has scored all WICKET POINTS is known as a ROVER. The rover can score the finishing stake point by hitting it. When time has run out in TIME-LIMIT tournament games, and neither side has scored all the points needed for victory, wicket (and stake) points are totalled at the end of the time-limit and the team with the most points is the winner.

## HOW PLAY IS MADE

Play is made by striking a ball with a mallet. The player who is doing this is called the STRIKER, and the ball that he strikes, the striker's ball. The striker may never strike an adversary's ball with his mallet. But by striking his ball against any other he is alive on, the striker may cause that ball to move/or score a point.

The players play each turn in the sequence shown on the STAKE. A player is initially entitled to one stroke in a turn, after which his turn ends unless in that stroke his ball has scored a wicket point or hit another ball. When the wicket is scored, the striker is entitled to play one additional or CONTINUATION STROKE. When another ball (whether opponent's or partner's) is hit, the striker is said to have made a ROQUET on that ball.

He then becomes DEAD on that ball and is entitled to two extra strokes. The first of these two strokes is known as the CRO-

QUET STROKE or TAKING CROQUET and is made after moving and placing the striker's ball in contact with or up to one mallet head away from the roqueted ball, which, if in contact in the croquet stroke, is known as the CROQUETED BALL. If in the croquet stroke the croqueted ball is sent off the court without first having made another roquet, the turn ends. During a turn the striker may roquet each ball he is ALIVE on once. He may make a further roquet on each ball provided that, since he has last roqueted it, his striker's ball has scored a wicket or upper stake point for itself and has thus cleared itself of its DEADNESS. Thus, by a series of strokes entitling him to continue, the striker may make one or more points, during one turn. Such a series is known as making a BREAK.

But CONTINUATION STROKES are not cumulative—you cannot run a wicket, hitting another ball in the process, and collect three strokes. Nor does running the first two (or any two) wickets earn more than one continuation stroke.

If a player first clears a wicket and then, on the same stroke, hits another ball, he may either take one continuation stroke and not be dead on the ball he's hit, or he may choose to roquet that ball and take two strokes. If a player makes a roquet as a consequence of a croquet stroke (if his ball not only moves the ball he's taking croquet on but goes on to hit yet another ball) he immediately takes croquet on that ball and continues to play. But if, during a croquet stroke, a player scores a wicket for his ball, he is entitled to only one continuation stroke, which is his reward for clearing the wicket.

A ball is said to be OUT-OF-BOUNDS when its vertical axis rolls more than halfway over the boundary. It is then known as a BALL-IN-HAND. This term is also used to describe a ball that has made a roquet, or any ball that must be picked up and moved.

After each stroke, all balls off the court are replaced one mallet head in from the point where they went out. This is also true of all balls within a mallet's head of the boundary line after each stroke, except the striker's ball. The balls are replaced a mallet head in from the line.

# SIX WICKET—ONE STAKE
# CROQUET COURT VARIATIONS

The regulation court shown is the layout used in national and international croquet tournaments. Regulation dimensions are shown. Where size and shape of lawn does not permit the full-scale layout, it may be scaled down to fit your lawn. Proportionately reduced court dimensions are shown on the diagram. The direction of play is indicated by the arrows in the illustrations.

| | BOUNDARY LINES | | CORNER WICKETS TO BOUNDARY LINES | | DISTANCE FROM BOUNDARY LINES TO CENTER STAKE | | DISTANCE FROM STAKE TO INFIELD WICKETS |
|---|---|---|---|---|---|---|---|
| | ENDS | SIDES | ENDS | SIDES | ENDS | SIDES | |
| (1) | 84 FT. | X 105 FT. | 21 FT. | X 21 FT. | 42 FT. | X 52½ FT. | 21 FT. |
| (2) | 60 FT. | X 74 FT. | 15 FT. | X 15 FT. | 30 FT. | X 37 FT. | 15 FT. |
| (3) | 42 FT. | X 52½ FT. | 10½ FT. | X 10½ FT. | 26 FT. | X 21 FT. | 10½ FT. |
| (4) | 30 FT. | X 37 FT. | 7½ FT. | X 7½ FT. | 15 FT. | X 18½ FT. | 7½ FT. |
| (5) | 21 FT. | X 26½ FT. | 5'4 FT. | X 5'4 FT. | 13 FT. | X 10½ FT. | 5'4 FT. |

STARTING TEE: 3 FEET IN FRONT OF WICKET NO. I FOR ALL SIZES ABOVE

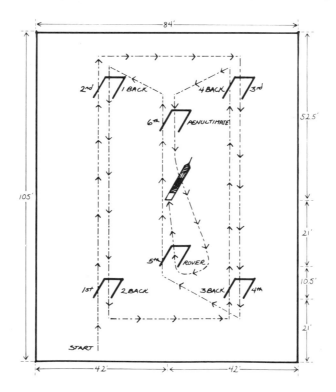

# NINE WICKET—TWO STAKE
# CROQUET COURT VARIATIONS

Croquet is the family fun game adaptable for play in almost any area. The nine wicket + two stake version may be enjoyed on a space as small as 20 ft in length and 10 ft in width or as large as 100 ft by 50 ft. Boundary lines should be made of string affixed to the four corners of the court.

By proportionately adjusting the dimensions as indicated on the chart many other court sizes can be set up and may even be modified to an L shape as illustrated.

DISTANCE BETWEEN

|  | COURT BOUNDARY LINES | | BOUNDARY LINES & STAKES | STAKES & WICKETS 1&7, 1&2, 6&7 | WICKETS 3,5,10,12 & SIDE BOUNDARIES |
|---|---|---|---|---|---|
|  | SIDES | ENDS |  |  |  |
| (1) | 100 FT | X 50 FT | 6 FT | 6 FT | 6 FT. |
| (2) | 80 FT | X 40 FT | 5 FT | 5 FT | 5 FT. |
| (3) | 20 FT | X 10 FT | 1 FT | 1½ FT | 1½ FT. |

STARTING TEE:  ONE-HALF THE DISTANCE BETWEEN THE STARTING STAKE AND THE NO. 1 WICKET

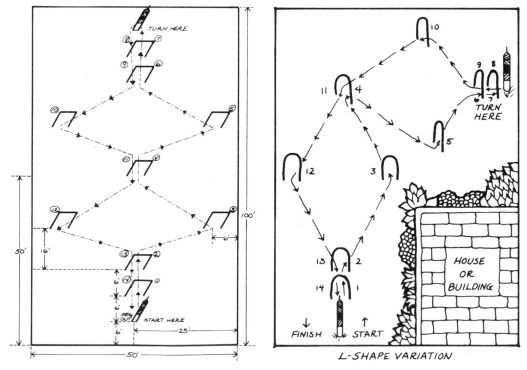

L-SHAPE VARIATION

# BASIC VERSIONS OF THE GAME

The basic rules of the traditional American nine wicket/two stake game *and* an introduction to the American six wicket/one stake sport of croquet including regulations for the following popular versions of play:

1. *Individual* (or one ball)
   For two to six players each playing one ball against the field.
2. *Singles* (four balls)
   Two players each playing two balls.
3. *Doubles* (four balls)
   Four players (in teams of two) each playing one ball.
4. *Triples* (six balls)
   Six players (in teams of three) each playing one ball.
   and
5. *Golf Croquet* (four or six balls)
   Two to six players.

The following basic rules apply to the first four versions above excluding Golf Croquet which will be treated separately. Where rules differ due to varying numbers of players, wickets and stakes, as well as court layout, we have provided a supplemental section covering specific points for each.

# BASIC RULES OF CROQUET

## USE OF MALLET

1. A player
   a) may hold any part of the mallet handle with one or both hands and may use any stance. (*i.e.*, center, side or golf).
   b) must hit the ball (not shove or push) with the striking end(s) of the mallet head only once per stroke (no double tap).
2. It shall be counted as a stroke if the mallet hits the wicket or ground but not the ball or misses the ball completely.
3. If a player, in attempting to strike his own ball, touches (with his foot or mallet) another ball, his turn ends and both balls are replaced.

4. The striker may not
   a) place another mallet against a ball and then hit it with his own.
   b) move or shake a ball by hitting a wicket or stake.
   c) touch or strike with his mallet any other ball than his own.

PENALTY for committing a fault under rules 1, 2, 3 & 4: End of Turn, with replacement of any balls having been moved.

## START OF PLAY

5. The toss of a coin (or lots drawn for individual play) determines the choice of order of play. A side may choose to play first or second and shall then play in the order shown on the stake.

6. All balls must start from the starting tee (from one mallet head to 3 feet—depending upon court length) behind the first wicket with each side playing alternative turns in the rotation indicated on the stake.

## MAKING A WICKET AND SCORING POINTS

7. A player's ball passing completely through the first (or first two) wicket(s) scores the wicket point(s) and is entitled to one additional stroke. One stroke (and wicket point) is earned for passing through each succeeding wicket in the order shown in the diagram.

8. If a player fails to run wicket number 1 on his first stroke, his turn ends.

9. A ball stopping in or rolling back into the wicket has not made the wicket nor scored the wicket point.

10. A ball is considered through the wicket when a straight edge placed against the approach side of the wicket does not touch the ball.

11. To score a wicket point, a ball must have *started* to run the wicket from the approach side.

12. A ball which is dead on another ball lying at or in the approach to the wicket may not hit that ball and if it does the wicket is not made, the player's turn ends and both balls are

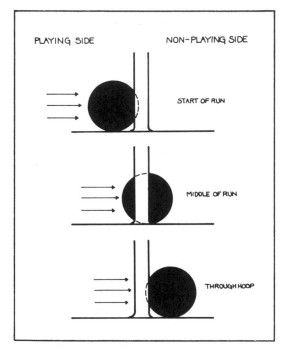

When a ball is through a wicket.

replaced.
  a) A ball which is dead on another ball lying beyond (not in-truding into) the wicket must make complete passage through the wicket, either before or after contact, to score the wicket point and receive one extra stroke.
13. A player may block (stymie) a wicket twice with a ball upon which the opponent is dead, but on the opponent's third turn he must leave the wicket clear or be lifted and replaced after that turn. A ball which is encroaching on the direct path through a wicket is considered to be a block or stymie.
14. In the Nine wicket game a ball hitting the turning stake scores a point, clears any prior deadness and earns one extra stroke to be played from where it comes to rest. (Not applicable in the six wicket game.)
  a) A rover ball hitting the finishing stake in its striker's turn (or put against it by another rover) scores the final point for that ball, which is removed from that game.

## ROQUET, CROQUET AND EXTRA STROKES

15. During a turn the striker is entitled to hit (ROQUET) each ball (either partner's or opponent's) that he is alive on and thereby earn two additional strokes. The stroker's ball then becomes dead on each ball so hit and may not hit it again until he scores his next wicket point for his ball.
    a) In hitting two or more balls upon which it is alive in the same stroke, the roquet will count on the first ball hit with the others being replaced.
    b) A ball which has made a roquet cannot, in that same stroke, score a wicket point.
16. If a striker's ball hits a ball on which it is dead, the striker's turn ends and both balls are replaced.
17. A striker's ball, after making a wicket, which then hits another ball in the same stroke may elect to:
    a) hit (roquet) the other ball to earn two strokes or
    b) not hit the other ball (and remain alive on it) and take on continuation stroke for having scored the wicket point. (The hit ball is not replaced.)
18. When a roquet is made, the striker's ball becomes a "ball-in-hand" and is brought to where the roqueted ball has come to rest in order to take the first (or CROQUET) stroke of the two it has earned.
19. In the croquet stroke the player may either:
    a) place his ball in contact with the roqueted ball and in striking it cause both balls to move (or shake) before taking his second shot or:
    b) place his ball against the roqueted ball and by holding his ball by foot or hand drive the other away and then play his second shot or:
    c) bring his own ball up to a mallet's head away from the roqueted ball and play his two strokes from there.
20. If in the croquet stroke the player plays his shot from a distance greater than a mallet's head from the ball hit OR if he loses contact with his balls during foot or hand shot, his turn is ended. All balls remain where they lie and no credit is given for wicket or stake points scored in that stroke.

21. If a ball is driven through its wicket by a ball which is alive on it in a roquet stroke or by another ball in its croquet stroke (a peel), that ball shall be counted as having scored the wicket point, is cleared of any deadness it may have had, but is not entitled to an extra stroke.

# OUT OF BOUNDS

22. A ball is out of bounds when its vertical axis crosses the boundary line (more than half way over). It shall be replaced on the court one mallet's head from where it first went out or, if near the corner, one mallet's head from the boundary lines.
23. When a player drives his ball through a wicket, so that it comes to rest out of bounds, his turn is ended and the ball shall be placed in bounds one mallet's head from where it went out.
24. At the end of every stroke all balls except the striker's less than a mallet's head from the boundary are placed that length from the line.
    a) If the space to which such a ball should be placed be occupied by another ball, the replaced ball shall be put up to a mallet's head in either direction from the said ball (but not touching) at the discretion of the striker.
    b) Should two balls be sent over the boundary or less than a mallet's head from the boundary at the same place, the ball first out of bounds or closest to it is placed first with the second placed as in a) above.
25. If in a roquet or croquet stroke any ball (except the striker's in the roquet stroke—see rule 26) goes out of bounds, the striker's turn ends and all balls on the court remain where they lie and all balls off the court placed one mallet's head in from the point on the boundary where they went off.
26. If, in making a roquet, the striker's ball goes out of bounds or caroms into a third ball (not the roqueted ball) sending it out, the latter ball is replaced with no penalty and the striker's ball is played as in rule 18.
27. If a ball is roqueted off the court by a striker's ball that is alive on it, the striker's turn ends but he remains alive on the ball so hit.

## PLAYING OUT OF TURN OR WRONG BALL

28. If a ball is played out of turn, all balls are replaced as at the beginning of play, and the play is resumed in proper sequence with the offending ball losing its next turn in that sequence.
29. If a player plays the wrong ball, his turn ends and all balls are replaced where they were before the fault occurred. In a singles game, a striker playing the wrong partner ball shall be considered to have played out of turn with the penalty as in Rule 28.

## INTERFERENCE, CALLING OR CONDONING FAULTS

30. If a ball is interfered with by an outside agent, except weather or accidentally by an opponent, in any way that materially affects the outcome of the stroke, that stroke shall be replayed. Otherwise, the ball shall be placed, as nearly as can be judged, where it would have come to rest, provided that no point or roquet can thereby be made. A rover ball prevented from scoring the stake by a staked-out ball shall be placed where it would otherwise have come to rest.
31. A fault or misplay by a player should be called as soon as it is discovered but must be called by his opponent before the next turn begins or else it will be automatically condoned.

## ROVER AND FINISHING THE GAME

32. A player who has made all the wickets in the proper sequence becomes rover and is considered alive on all balls.
33. Assuming he is alive on them, a rover ball may hit any other ball only once per turn.
34. After hitting at least two balls, a rover ball may be cleared of deadness by passing through any wicket in any direction (or by hitting the turning stake in the 9 wicket game) and thus earn one continuation stroke.
35. Upon being cleared of deadness on two or three balls, a rover ball may not hit the last ball he was dead on until he hits

another ball first whereupon the temporary deadness is also cleared.

36. A rover that runs a wicket in clearing its deadness and in the same stroke hits a ball upon which it was last dead incurs no penalty, and unless either ball is driven out of bounds, both balls remain where they lie and the striker is entitled to take his continuation stroke.

37. A rover's ball may only be driven into the stake (either on a roquet or croquet stroke) by another rover which is alive on it, whereupon it will be considered to have finished the game (and scored a point for itself), and shall be immediately removed from the court.

38. A rover ball roqueted into the stake by a striker's ball which is dead on it shall be replaced and considered still in play.

39. A rover ball hitting the stake after making a roquet is not staked out and shall play normally off the roqueted ball.

40. When one ball of a side has staked out of the game it is removed from the court immediately and play continues in the proper rotation with the staked out ball losing all subsequent turns.

41. If in a roquet shot a striker's rover ball drives another rover ball into the stake, it is removed from play and the striker receives two strokes taken a mallet's head in any direction from the stake.

42. The game is won by the side that finishes the game with both balls first, or in a time limit game by the side scoring the highest total of wicket or stake points.

## STRATEGY

Along with the basic objective of scoring all the wicket and stake points first, each team or player (in singles) should employ those offensive or defensive moves which will restrict the progress of the opponents. Defensive tactics include separating opponent's balls, thus forcing him to take long shots to strike other balls—taking an opponent out of position to make his next wicket (particularly when that ball is "dead" on his partner's ball). An opponent who is "dead" on two or three balls and can be kept that way has lost considerable offensive capabilities.

The primary offensive tactic is to utilize as many balls (both partner's and opponent's) as can be brought into setting a "Break" in order to score as many wicket points in one turn as possible. By skillful use and placement of two or three other balls at wickets ahead of the striker's next wicket in proper sequence he can make up to eleven wickets in one "all round break" during his turn. This optimum feat in croquet is the equivalent of a grand slam homer in baseball or running the table in pool.

Defensive strategy frequently involves partner's balls joining up on the boundary line far from their opponents to avoid providing them an opportunity to pick up a break for their side. This move often baffles spectators since it appears that no one is attempting to go for wicket points. It is often the case of discretion being the better part of valor. All tactical decisions involve weighing the risk of each move (in terms of each player's ability) against the reward if the move succeeds. To many this is the essential challenge of Croquet.

# GOLF CROQUET

Golf Croquet is the one version of the game which is played by all croquet playing countries in the world with only minor court oriented differences in the rules.

The surprising thing is that it is not REAL croquet since the "croquet stroke" is never used. Its popularity rests in the fact that it is easy to learn, gives excellent practice in some basic strokes such as running wickets and roquet or hit shots, as well as teaching the sequence of play and route of wickets on the court. Since it can be played in a relatively short period of time, it is useful when many people wish to play, such as in one day tournaments.

## OBJECTIVES OF GOLF CROQUET

Golf Croquet is a game in which the winner of a wicket is the side that makes that wicket in the fewest number of strokes. The similarity with golf is that everyone is going for the same wicket at any one time. The important difference is that the balls are allowed to interfere with each other.

The balls are paired as in croquet—and doubles, trebles or singles may be played. A point is scored when one side manages to run a wicket in its proper order with either of its balls; (the winning side in a timed game is that which has scored the most points when time is called.)

The balls are played strictly in sequence—like croquet; there are no extra shots or turns for making a roquet or running a wicket. For example, if red makes a wicket all players then turn their attention to the next wicket and black has the first shot in approaching that wicket.

# RULES OF GOLF CROQUET

In the United States, as in the United Kingdom, golf croquet is played on a 6-wicket, 1-stake court layout as outlined below. It may, however, be played on a 9-wicket, 2-stake court by modifying the direction of play.

The rules relating to singles doubles and triples play apply subject to the following modifications:

## THE COURSE

a) Balls are played into the game from one mallet's length from the center stake. In a short version, 7 points are contested: the first 6 and number 1 again for the seventh point.
b) When 13 points are contested, the first 12 points are as in croquet. The thirteenth point is the third wicket.
c) When nineteen points are contested, the wickets 1-back to the rover are contested twice before contesting the third wicket. The stake is not contested.

## THE GAME

a) All balls are always for the same wicket in order. The point is scored for the side whose ball first runs the wicket. The game ends as soon as one side has scored a majority of the points to be played (*i.e.*, 4 out of 7 in the short game). It is customary to keep the tally of the score as in match play golf by declaring a side to be one or more points up or down or all square as the case may be.

b) Each turn consists of one stroke. The rules relating to roquet, croquet and continuation strokes do not apply.

c) The balls are played in the same sequence and color combinations for sides as in basic croquet.

## RUNNING A HOOP

If a striker causes one of the balls of his side to partly run a wicket during a stroke, such a ball must begin to run such a wicket again before it can be scored by that ball in any subsequent stroke. But if an adversary causes a ball partly to run a wicket during a stroke such a ball may run that wicket in a subsequent stroke. If a ball runs two wickets in one stroke, it scores both wickets for its side. The wicket point is scored by a ball that is cannoned, peeled or roqueted through a wicket except that a partner ball which has failed to clear the wicket on its own stroke may not be so driven through by his partner unless that ball was put into the wicket by an opponent.

## JUMP SHOT

A player may not deliberately make his ball rise from the ground. If he does so accidentally, or in ignorance of this law, and in consequence runs a wicket for his striker's or partner's ball, the point shall not be scored. Likewise, if as a consequence thereof any balls are displaced, such balls may be replaced at the option of the adversary side.

## ADVANCING A BALL PREMATURELY FOR THE NEXT POINT

A player must play so as to contest the wicket in its proper order rather than seek to gain an advantage for the next wicket in order. But a player contesting the wicket in order by, for example, attempting to cannon another ball, may legitimately play the stroke at the strength calculated to bring his ball to rest nearer the next wicket in order.

## PLAYING OUT OF TURN OR WITH A WRONG BALL

If the striker plays out of turn or with the wrong ball, that stroke and any subsequent strokes are null and void. All balls shall be replaced: the right ball shall be played by the correct player, and the other balls shall follow in due sequence. No points made during the period of error shall be scored.

These rules, while USCA-approved, do not correspond exactly to the "A-Level" rules used in tournament play. Each year, the USCA publishes an updated pamphlet of advanced American rules. If you wish to get serious about American croquet, you should contact:

> The United States Croquet Association
> 500 Avenue of Champions
> Palm Beach Gardens, Florida 33418-9990
> (305) 627-3999

The British Association game is played in all other countries where croquet is a competitive sport. For those interested in expanding their croquet horizons, there is *The Laws of Association and Golf Croquet.*

Contact:

> The American Croquet Association
> 4735 North 32nd Place
> Phoenix, Arizona
> (602) 955-1547

Or contact:

> The Croquet Association
> The Hurlingham Club
> London SW 6, England

If you wish to start a college team, you can contact either the ACA or NECCA:

> The New England Croquet Association
> 372 Harvard Street
> Cambridge, Massachusetts 02138
> (617) 492-6141

Dr. Xandra Kayden's witty pamphlet, *The Basics of Croquet,* is also available through NECCA.

# *Glossary*

**A-Class Player:** A scratch player in American competition; In England, a player with a handicap of two or better.

**Advanced Play (Laws of):** The suggested "A Level" rules of the United States Croquet Association.

**Alive:** In American play, a ball which has cleared a wicket but has not roqueted a ball is said to be alive. In the British game, all balls are alive at the start of every turn.

**All-Round Break:** Running all the hoops in a single turn.

**American Roque League:** Formed in 1916, it is the "Supreme Court" of roque, with chapters from coast to coast.

**American System:** The method of organizing a tournament that guarantees each player a number of games, by blocking them and having each play the others within his block.

**Angle of Divergence:** Angle at which balls part when a croquet shot is made.

**Angle of Split:** On a croquet shot, the angle between two lines, along which the two balls travel.

**Association Croquet:** British rules used throughout all the countries (excluding the United States) which play tournament croquet. Many Americans play both Association and USCA rules.

**Aunt Emma:** A conservative player who wastes his or her talent through dull and uninspired play.

**Back Peel:** Peeling a ball through its own hoop, immediately after you have run that hoop.

**Baire:** A game played in 7th century Ireland; possibly a primitive form of croquet.

**Ball In Hand:** A ball that has to be picked up and moved, either before taking croquet or because it has gone out-of-bounds.

**Basket:** Crossed center wickets once used in garden croquet. It also refers to the area of the center arches in roque.

**Baulk-Line:** On each of the short sides of the yard-line are other unmarked lines, approximately twelve yards in length, known as the baulk-lines. In British play, these are, in effect, the starting lines.

**B-Class Player:** A +2 handicap player in America; in England, one with a handicap of between 2-1/2 and 6.

**Beefy Shot:** A long, hard shot.

**Being Off Color:** The opposite of hitting true.

**Beugelspel:** A Dutch game that is similar to croquet and its forerunner pall mall.

**Big Handicap:** An all-comer's event, usually held during British club tournaments.

**Bisque:** A unit of difference between two player's handicaps, it is the number of extra turns given to the player with the highest handicap.

**Bisque Extraction:** Strategy of making your opponent use up his bisques ineffectively or for defensive purposes only.

**Bombard:** The croquet shot in roque.

**Break:** The method of extending your turn by using one or more of the other balls.

**Break Down:** To err so that your turn involuntarily comes to an end during the course of a break.

**British Open Championship:** British singles title, played annually at Roehampton.

141

**Cage:** Another name for crossed wickets, an arrangement used in garden croquet.

**Camanachd:** Scotch Gaelic for hurley, a game similar to baire and hockey.

**Cannon Shot:** To make a roquet on the same stroke as a croquet shot, that is, to make a croqueted ball hit another.

**Carrying Through:** Following through with your arms leading; term coined by Lord Tollemache.

**C-Class Player:** A player with a handicap of greater than six (in England), or greater than two in the United States.

**Center Style:** Traditional stance with mallet between-the-knees.

**Cleaning Yourself:** Becoming "undead" by running a hoop or, in England, becoming alive at the end of your turn.

**Clips:** The color of each ball, these are placed on the hoops to mark the player's progress.

**Cluiche:** The Irish word for play; it is pronounced "crooky."

**Cold Ball:** The roque, the last played ball of your opponent.

**Condoning:** Failure of a player to claim a foul within the limit of claims makes the play in question valid, with no foul charged to the striker.

**Consignificant Crouching:** An archaic etymological form of "croquet."

**Contact:** To touch or make contact with another ball.

**Continuation Stroke:** The extra stroke earned by running a hoop; also earned when a roquet is made, it is used after first taking croquet.

**Corner:** To hit your ball into a corner for defensive purposes.

**Corner Balls:** Balls sent off the court that are returned to a point within one yard of a corner (English).

**Corner Cannon Shot:** Combination of rush and croquet stroke; you roquet a ball after taking croquet from another ball that is in the corner.

**Corner Flags:** Placed at the four corners of the course; seldom used in the United States.

**Corner Pegs:** These are placed a yard on each side of each flag.

**Count Upon:** In roque, you are said to count upon another ball when you make contact with it.

**Coupe Croquet:** A parlor game which combines billiards and marbles.

**Crochet:** An old French dialect form of "croquet."

**Crooky:** An old Irish game, claimed by some to be a forerunner of croquet.

**Croquet Association:** Founded as the All England Croquet Club, it is now the world's governing body (with the exception of the United States).

**Croquet Carnival:** Tournaments held annually by the Australian Croquet Association. Among the events are the Interstate Cup Competition and the English Medal Event.

**Croquet Golf (Golf Croquet):** A variation of croquet in which the hoops are treated as if they were holes in golf.

**Croquet Stroke:** The stroke you earn after making roquet. Your ball is placed against the roqueted ball, and in taking croquet, you send both your own ball and the croqueted ball to desired positions.

**Cross Peg:** A leave in which the enemy balls are left straddling the peg, thus preventing or impeding your foe's intended shot.

**Cross Wire:** A leave in which the enemy balls are left on each side of a hoop, thus preventing your foe from taking his desired shot.

**Crown:** The top part of a hoop (the crossbar).

**Crush Shot:** A crush shot occurs when, in attempting to jar a ball through its hoop, the striker makes simultaneous contact with the mallet, ball and wicket upright. This shot can happen when a ball is too close to the wicket, and can sometimes be anticipated. It is an illegal shot, but tricky to call.

**Cut Rush:** A shot played so that the rushed ball moves off at an angle to the direction of the stroke.

**Deadness:** When you hit another ball with your own, you can no longer use that ball for the duration of your turn (except for the croquet shot), until running a hoop in the American game, or for British play, until the end of your turn.

**Deadness Board:** Implement used to keep track of who is dead on which ball.

**Delayed Triple Peel:** Abandoning a triple peel temporarily, to be resumed later in your turn.

**Destroy Shot:** A shot hit with unusual force in order to send a croqueted ball the largest distance possible; an American term.

**Double Banking:** Playing two games on the same lawn simultaneously, due to space or time shortage; the games are completely separate.

**Double Elimination:** Type of tournament in which a player must lose two matches before being eliminated.

**Double Peel:** A ball knocked through two hoops in the same turn, but not necessarily on two successive strokes.

**Double Roll:** A shot in which the striker's ball travels the same distance as the croqueted ball.

**Double Tap:** A fault in which the striker's ball is hit twice during the same swing.

**Double Target:** Two balls so placed, or a ball and a hoop so grouped, that the effective target area is doubled.

**Draw:** One of the two competition cards used in the two-life system of determining the matches in a tournament event.

**Drive Shot:** By hitting very slightly down on your ball during a croquet shot, your foe's ball will go roughly three times farther than your own.

**English Medal Event:** A part of the Croquet Carnival in which ten players from each Australian state compete for medals donated by the Croquet Association of England.

**Fair Position:** In roque, a ball that has properly cleared its hoop is said to be in fair position.

**Fault:** An unacceptable, or foul stroke.

**Feather-Off:** A light take-off shot.

**Foot Shot:** A croquet shot taken with your foot on your ball. Now illegal in American standard play.

**Forestalling:** If you foul and your opponent does not stop play before your next stroke to claim a misplay, no penalty is assessed, and the foul is said to be forestalled.

**Four-Ball Break:** The backbone of the game, a play in which all four balls are used to maneuver your way around the court, ideally in a single turn.

**Free Shot:** A shot which, if missed, will not immediately have any dangerous consequences.

**Full-Bisque Play:** A variety of handicap play in which the players are allowed to use all of their respective bisques, as opposed to the standard system which allows only the inferior player to use bisques.

**Garden Croquet:** Amateur, unofficial, backyard croquet; the most popular and well-known variety of the sport. Usually played with nine wickets and two stakes.

**Golf Style:** Style of swinging in which the mallet is swung across the body like a putter.

**Go To Bed With Bisques:** To lose in a handicap game with one or more unused bisques.

**Hale Setting:** Introduced in 1872, a court arrangement with six hoops and two pegs; replaced by the Willis Setting.

**Half-Bisque:** An extra shot used in handicap doubles and some singles, in which you cannot score points; hence they are used for maneuvering the ball. British.

**Half-Jump Shot:** By hitting down on the ball, you try to drive both your ball and the obstructing ball through the hoop.

**Hidden Ball:** A roque term, this is a ball that cannot be hit by the enemy without a foul stroke or bank shot, due to its position on the court.

**Hitting True:** Hitting the ball with a level swing, as opposed to hitting up or down.

**Holden, 'Doc' Milton Trophy:** Awarded to Eastern Seaboard Singles Champion.

**Home Run:** In roque, when a ball scores all of its points in a single turn, it has made a home run.

**Hong Kong:** Archaic term for taking croquet.

**Hoop-Bound:** When one's swing is impeded by a hoop.

**Hoop-Running Shot:** A shot through your proper hoop.

**Hot Ball:** In roque, foe's next played ball.

**Hurlingham Club:** London club, site of the British Open Championship and the Croquet Association.

**Innings:** When the balls are arranged so that you are more likely to score points than your opponent, you are said to be "in," and thus have the innings. In roque, an inning is a full turn by all the players.

**Interstate Cup:** Known also as the Eire Cup, the object of an annual competition held between the six states of Australia.

**Irish Grip:** A grip with the palms of both hands held away from the body; it originated with the great Irish players of the Edwardian Era.

**Irish Peel:** A roll stroke which is similar to a half-jump shot, in that both balls go through their wickets.

**Irish Style:** Similar to the center style, but using the Irish grip.

**Is For:** The next hoop that a ball must run, e.g. "yellow is for third hoop."

**Jam:** An illegal shot made with unlawfully prolonged contact between the ball and the arch when a ball lies against a hoop; similar to a carry in volleyball.

**Jaws:** Entrance to the uprights of a hoop.

**Join Up:** To play your ball to a spot near its partner ball.

**Jump Ball:** By hitting down on your ball, you can make it jump over an obstructing ball.

**King Ball:** Ball in royal roque that supersedes the rover ball.

**Kiss Cannon:** Like a corner cannon shot except for the added element of hitting a third ball with the croqueted ball, as well as roqueting your intended target with your own ball.

**Knock-Out:** An elimination system in tournaments in which a single loss means elimination.

**Knocking-Up:** Hitting practice balls to get the lie of a course.

**Lag:** Method of determining the right of choice in roque and garden croquet; like the one used in pool.

**Lay Up:** A long, wild or reckless shot; made to escape from a dangerous position or to waste a shot when you are uncertain as to your next move.

**Laying a Break:** Positioning balls at future hoops to set up a possible break.

**Level Play:** Non-handicap competition.

**Lift:** Any situation that calls for picking up a ball, as in prior to taking croquet, or when a ball is driven out of bounds.

**Limit of Claims:** Time during which a fault can be called, or else it is invalid.

**Long Bisquer:** Player with a high handicap.

**Longman Cup:** Trophy given annually since 1926 to winners of the handicap competition among croquet clubs in England.

**Lower Stake:** The near stake in the American nine-wicket layout, and the eighth and sixteenth points in a roque course.

**Macrobertson International Shield:** International competition held every four years since 1925; involves England (with the most wins), New Zealand, and Australia.

**McGowan Trophy:** An award given by the American Roque League.

**Moreton-In-The-Marsh:** A town in Western England which was the site of the first all-comers' tournament.

**National Croquet Association:** American group formed in 1882, at the nadir of croquet's popularity, it helped spark new interest in the sport. Now defunct.

**National Regulation Croquet:** An American game which is a combination of croquet and roque, and is played on a roque court.

**Net Points:** The total number of points scored minus the total number of points scored against; they are used to break ties under the American System in Britain, if the number of games won are tied.

**Next-Two Leave:** A leave whereby you leave your partner with a rush to his hoop and one enemy ball at each of the next two hoops for your future use.

**No Brainer:** A lucky shot.

**Non-Playing Side:** Area behind a hoop as you approach that wicket from the proper direction.

**Norwich, Connecticut:** Entry point of croquet from Europe into the United States, it was the site of rule revisions in 1899.

**Off The ...:** When you score a hoop off a certain ball, you are said to have made it, for example, "off the red."

**Official Handicap Book:** Contains handicaps of all players registered with England's Croquet Association.

**Official Regulation Croquet:** American game which is a combination of roque and croquet. Sanctioned by the American Roque League; it should not be confused with lawn croquet as played under U.S.C.A. rules.

**One-Ball Shot:** A shot in which only one ball is hit.

**Out Player:** The player who does not have the innings.

**Pall Mall:** An early version of croquet that was a favorite of Charles II; also spelled *paille maille* and *pesle mesle*.

**Pass Roll:** A croquet shot in which you send your ball farther than the croqueted ball.

**Peel:** Causing a ball other than your own to run its proper hoop.

**Peg Down:** To interrupt a game, marking the position of the balls and clips, with the intention of resuming later.

**Pegged-Out Game:** Game in which at least one ball has been pegged-out.

**Penultimate:** The next-to-last hoop.

**Pig Pen:** The crossed center wickets occasionally used in nine-wicket croquet. Also known as "the basket."

**Pilot Ball:** The ball off which you make a hoop in a four-ball break.

**Pioneer Ball:** In a three- or four-ball break, the ball that is sent forward to the hoop after the one you are going for.

**Pivot Ball:** The middle ball in a four-ball break; it is placed near the peg on the side you are then playing.

**Playing Line:** A line on a roque court that corresponds to the yardline on a British course.

**Playing Side:** Area in front of a hoop as your ball approaches it.

**Plaza-Toro Technique:** Miller and Thorp's term for letting yourself be carried by your mallet instead of carrying through with your arms leading; named for the Duke of Plaza-Toro, who liked to lead his regiment from behind.

**Predominance:** A common error in which one hand or foot leads your swing too much.

**President's Cup:** Major British tournament for the United Kingdom's best eight players; played with a 1/16th inch clearance of ball through hoop, instead of the usual 1/8th inch.

**Process:** Along with the draw, one of two competition cards used in determining the line-up and seeding for tournament events.

**Pseudo-Cannon Shot:** A three-ball croquet shot in which you move the croqueted ball just a little way out of the corner.

**Pull:** The tendency in a croquet shot for the balls to curve in an inward manner from their line of aim.

**Push:** Keeping the mallet on the ball for an appreciable time after hitting it; it is allowed only on a croquet shot—so long as your mallet does not speed up when in contact with the ball.

**Quadruple Peel:** A four-wicket peel.

**Qualifying Shot:** The shot which begins your turn.

**Queen Ball:** The neutral ball in royal roque.

**Questionable Stroke:** A play of dubious legality, or in which there is a great chance of a foul; on such a controversial play, the contestants should consult the referee before the shot is made.

**Quintuple Peel:** A rarely seen five-wicket peel.

**Referee on Appeal:** An English term for requesting the referee to rule on a controversy after the act has occurred.

**Referee on Call:** On some plays, such as a questionable stroke, the referee should be requested to act on the controversy before the play in question occurs; also an English term.

**Reverse Palm Grip:** The most popular grip, it is made with the lower hand's palm away from the body and the upper hand's knuckles away from the body.

**Right of Choice:** After a lag or a toss of a coin, the winner has the option of choosing starting position or choice of balls.

**Rigor Mortis:** Being dead on all balls, and therefore unable to move with the assistance of the other balls for the duration of your turn; also known as three ball dead or three B D.

**Roehampton:** One of England's most famous croquet clubs, it is the home of the Roehampton Rovers and the Roehampton League.

**Roehampton League:** The Roehampton team challenges other clubs in this competition, and this, as well as the growth of English university teams has helped the expansion of inter-club competition in the United Kingdom.

**Roehampton Rovers:** The Roehampton Club's team in the league named after it.

**Roll Stroke:** A croquet shot used to add distance to the flight of your own ball as well as the croqueted ball, it is taken with a downward sweep instead of a level swing.

**Roque News Two-Ball Trophy:** Given to roque's national two-ball champion.

**Roquet:** When a ball is hit and made to hit another ball (either deliberately or by accident); it is generally followed by a croquet shot and continuation stroke.

**Routledge's Handbook of Croquet:** English publication written by Edmund Routledge in 1861. Probably the first rule book, and with numerous modifications, basically still governs croquet.

**Rover Ball:** One that has passed through all the hoops but has not yet hit the final peg; it can make moves on all other balls in a given turn, as deadness does not apply to the rover.

**Rover Hoop:** The last hoop before the final peg.

**Royal Roque:** A variation of roque which features a neutral white ball, called the queen ball, and a king ball, which supercedes a rover ball.

**Rush (Long or Short):** A roquet shot which sends the roqueted ball in a given direction.

**Rush Line:** An imaginary line along which a ball is roqueted on a rush shot.

**Rush Line Principle:** The shot made before an intended rush shot should be taken from a spot on or near the rush line.

**Scatter:** A shot played only as a last resort which separates balls that lie too close together.

**Schedule of Bisques:** The number of bisques awarded according to the type of event.

**Scratch Player:** As in golf, a croquet player with a handicap of zero.

**Sextuple Peel:** Part of a plan to finish the game in two breaks; similar to a quadruple peel, just extended. J.W. Solomon is renowned for making two successful sextuple peels to win an Open championship.

**Shepherding:** Illegal ploy of letting your mallet guide your ball through the hoop by a push rather than by a legal stroke.

**Side:** Technique in which the ball is not struck with the center of your mallet; used for cut rushes or for making awkward wickets.

**Split:** A roque term for making contact with a ball and causing it to move; in roque, shots that are not splits are direct shots.

**Split Shot:** A croquet shot in which both balls go off at different angles. Similar to splits in billiards or pool.

**Spread Wickets:** A garden arrangement whereby you separate certain wickets for added difficulty.

**Stalk:** Walking up behind a ball in the line you wish to send it, in order to insure proper aim.

**Stepping Stone:** When your ball is placed near a hoop or the peg, in a position that is advantageous to your partner.

**Sticky Wicket:** Having a difficult approach to a hoop, or being stuck in a hoop; also the name of a bi-annual croquet tournament held in Centre Isle, Oyster Bay, N.Y.

**Stop Shot:** By delivering an upward blow to one's own ball on a croquet shot, you drive the croqueted ball a considerable distance, while your ball barely moves.

**Straight Croquet:** A shot in which the striker's ball goes half the distance of the croqueted ball.

**Straight Triple Peel:** Doing three peels with the backward ball making the same three hoops.

**Striker:** Player whose turn it is.

**Stroke:** Any movement of the mallet that deliberately or otherwise results in movement of the ball.

**Stymie:** A ball blocking the intended path of your own ball.

**Surrey Cup:** A championship held at Cheltenham in the same week in September as the President's Cup Tourney, for the next best eight United Kingdom players (behind those who competed for the President's Cup).

**Take-Off Shot:** A croquet shot in which the croqueted ball moves a little, but the striker's ball moves a great distance.

**Thick Take-Off:** A croquet shot in which the croqueted ball moves a somewhat greater distance than on a simple take-off, and the striker's ball goes a considerable distance.

**Three-Ball Break:** Break using three balls, it is the corner-stone of the pegged-out game.

**Tice:** A shot which places your ball in a position where your foe is likely to shoot at it, but your ball is a sufficient distance from your foe that he is likely to miss should he attempt it.

**Two-Ball Break:** Break using two balls, it is the most difficult of all the breaks, as it involves shots of the greatest distance.

**Two-Life System:** Method of setting up competition in a tournament, using draw and process cards, it has the asset of mixing byes and matches throughout the card.

**United States Croquet Association:** Governing body for the sport of American croquet.

**Up the Country:** Another name for taking croquet.

**Upright Style:** Another name for the front style of swinging your mallet outside your feet, which gives you greater freedom of movement and additional power.

**Victoria Park Electric Light Carnival:** Sponsored by the Western Australian Croquet Association, it features croquet played every night from January 28 to February 22.

**Waive:** To pass your turn.

**Wall Shot:** In roque a shot used in which you carom your ball off the surrounding wall when you are unable to make a direct shot on your intended target.

**Widow Ball:** In roque, a three-ball variety with a neutral ball called the widow ball.

**Willis Setting:** Introduced in 1922, it is the present-day court arrangement using one center peg and six hoops.

**Winter Wickets:** Thin wickets used when the ground is hard or frozen.

**Wired Ball:** A ball behind a wicket or peg that cannot be hit by the striker's ball or other ball because of the obstruction.

**Yard-Line Area:** On an English court, an unmarked area surrounding the playing field which includes two baulk-lines.

**Yard-Line Ball:** In British play, a ball that is sent out of bounds and is replaced on the yard-line at a point where it left the court.

**G. Nigel Aspinall**

# Records and Rosters

## HISTORICAL ROSTER OF CROQUET PLAYERS

**Arnold, Bobby:** Seven-time American roque champion.

**Aspinall, G. Nigel:** One of the top world players presently competing. A Briton, he currently holds the only −5 handicap. Aspinall is the current British Open Champion and winner of the President's cup.

**Beaton, R.C.J.:** Two-time winner of British Open Title and four-time mixed doubles winner. An outstanding United Kingdom player of the 1920's and 1930's.

**Bray, Roger:** One of the better players currently competing, this Englishman once held a −5 handicap.

**Clark, Ed:** Six-time American roque champion, he won his last two titles thirteen years apart. From Springfield, Massachusetts.

**Corbally, Cyril:** A great Irish player, he introduced new skills and tactics into croquet, aiding in the game's resurgence from 1890 to World War I.

**Cotter, E.P.C.:** Outstanding British player and author, frequent doubles partner of J.W. Solomon.

**Crane, Mrs. V.C.:** Current Australian champion, from Victoria.

**Crosby, Samuel:** Helped form the American Roque League, and is responsible for coining the word "roque."

**Drummond, Capt.:** Founded England's Croquet Association with Walter Peel.

**Duke of Marlborough:** Formerly the unoffocial social leader of the Southampton, Long Island, N.Y. croquet set.

**Dupre, Lt. Col. W.B.:** Outstanding United Kingdom croquet player of the 1920's and 1930's; frequent doubles partner of D.D. Steel.

**Elvey, Rev. G.F. Handel:** Croquet author, he was president of England's croquet Association in the 1940's and 1950's.

**Goldwyn, Samuel:** Famed Hollywood producer and croquet aficionado, he installed a sand-trap on his home course to thwart the likes of Louis Jourdan and Darryl F. Zanuck.

**Hicks, Humphrey O.:** Five-time British Open winner since 1932, he was the holder of the lowest handicap ever, −5½; he plays with an unorthodox side-style.

**Jacobus, Charles:** Winner of roque competition at 1904 Olympics in St. Louis, he is the sport's only Olympic champion.

**Jacques, John:** An enterprising young Englishman, he was probably the first to manufacture croquet equipment. The company he established is now the world's oldest sporting goods manufacturer.

**Joad, Mrs.:** First winner of the Women's Championship for croquet in England, in 1869.

**Jourdan, Louis:** Perhaps the most talented croquet player among the celebrity set.

**Marx, Harpo:** Along with the Algonquin Set he helped popularize croquet in the United States in the 1920's through 1940's.

**Matthews, P.D. "Duff":** Along with Leslie O'Callaghan and Cyril Corbally, one of the great Irish players who helped revitalize the game before World War I.

**O'Callaghan, Leslie:** One of the triumvirate of great Irish players before the first World War.

**Oddie, Miss N.:** Frequent mixed doubles partner of John Solomon, 1954 English mixed doubles winner.

**Ormerod, Dr. W.:** 1975 doubles winner with G. Nigel Aspinall, once held a − 5 handicap. Author of a croquet book and present head of the British Croquet Association.

**Osborn, Jack:** Founder, Executive Director of the United States Croquet Association, he is a top-ranked American player over the last fifteen years of competition.

**Peck, Archie:** A highly-ranked American player. President, Palm Beach Croquet Club. Director of U.S.C.A.

**Peel, Walter:** Early champion (1868) who founded England's Croquet Association with Captain Drummond.

**Prentis, Ted:** One of the top American players; former Eastern U.S. Singles titleist, a member of the Westhampton Mallet Club and New York Croquet Club; Director U.S.C.A.

**Reckitt, Geoffrey:** One of the great British players and authorities on croquet.

**Reid, Captain Mayne A.:** American boys' author and Mexican War hero who helped popularize croquet with his 1863 book.

**Robertson, Sir MacPherson:** Donated MacRobertson Shield in 1925 to the Croquet Association for international test matches held every four to six years between England, Australia and New Zealand.

**Ross, Arthur G.:** A New Zealander, he is an eleven-time New Zealand champion and respected authority on the game.

**Routledge, Edmund:** Author of Routledge's Handbook on Croquet, probably the game's first rule book.

**Rounds, W.A.:** First president of the American Roque League, he also incorporated that group.

**Shipman, A.G.:** The first American croquet champion in 1882; from New York City.

**Solomon, John W.:** The "Babe Ruth" of croquet, with more than fifty titles to his credit; presently holds a handicap of − 4; has the most international appearances and the most wins in international competition.

**Steel, D.D.:** Fifteen-time womens' champion, four-time British Open champion and holder of seven mixed doubles titles, she was perhaps the foremost woman player in the history of the sport.

**Stephens, Wayne:** Seven-time American roque champion.

**Strachan, Douglas:** Irish champion during the 1960's, he is a member of England's Hurlingham Club.

**Swope, Herbert Jr.:** One of the top-rated American players, his father helped popularize croquet in this country as part of the Algonquin Set. Co-founder and former president N.Y.C.C. and Director U.S.C.A.

**Tankoos, S. Joseph:** One of the better American players, he was the chairman of the New York Croquet Club.

**Tollemache, Baron John Lyonel:** A famous English croquet player and author, his book is possibly the longest on the subject of croquet.

**Whitmore, Walter-Jones:** Winner of the first British Open championship, he invented new rules for the game (both of which declined in popularity). He was the first to attempt a codification of rules and devise a system of tactics for croquet.

**Windsor, M.S.:** A great Australian champion, with five appearances in Mac-Robertson Shield Competition, he is now a manufacturer of high-level croquet equipment.

**Woollcott, Alexander:** A major croquet advocate, the author, playwright and raconteur had his own course at Neshobe Island in Vermont.

**Wylie, Keith:** A top player, he used champagne corks to lighten his mallets.

**Zanuck, Darryl F.:** Hollywood producer and one of the sport's great devotees, he had his own elaborate course in Palm Springs.

# U.S. CROQUET HALL OF FAME

*Each year, the Croquet Foundation of America*
*inducts into the U.S. Croquet Hall of Fame*
*those who have done the most for the sport in America.*

George Abbott
Paul Butler
Margaret Emerson
Raoul Fleischmann
Andrew Fuller
Samuel Goldwyn
John David Griffin
William Harbach
W. Averell Harriman
Moss Hart
Howard Hawks
William Hawks
Milton "Doc" Holden
Louis Jourdan
George S. Kaufman
John Lavalle
Mrs. Carvel (Susie) Linden
Tom Lufkin
Duncan McMartin
Hilda McMartin
Jean Negulesco

Elizabeth B. Newell
Jack R. Osborn
Richard Pearman
J. Archie Peck
Mrs. Ogden (Lilian) Phipps
Edmund A. Prentis, III
Richard Rodgers
Mrs. Richard (Dorothy) Rodgers
Michael Romanoff
George Sanders
Herbert Bayard Swope, Jr.
Herbert Bayard Swope, Sr.
Catherine Tankoos
S. Joseph Tankoos
Francis O. Tayloe
Alexander Woollcott
Gig Young
John Young
Nelga Young
Darryl F. Zanuck

# UNITED STATES CROQUET ASSOCIATION
# TOP TEN GRAND PRIX RANKING

## 1983

1. Prentis, T.
2. Osborn, J. C.
3. Arnett, R. B.
4. Burchfield, A.
5. Jones, K.
6. Osborn, J. R.
7. Dribben, D.
8. Pearman, R.
9. Peck, A.
10. Bell, R.

## 1984

1. Osborn, J. C.
2. Jones, K.
3. Bell, R.
4. Bast, J.
5. Young, J.
6. Osborn, J. R.
7. Pearman, R.
8. Dribben, D.
9. Illingworth R.
10. Peck, A.

## 1985

1. Osborn, J. C.
2. Osborn, J. R.
3. Bell, R.
4. Erwin, J.
5. Young, J.
6. Degnan, D.
7. Dribben, D.
8. Prentis, D.
9. Burchfield, A.
10. Young, N.

## 1986

1. Osborn, J. C.
2. Prentis, D.
3. Erwin, J.
4. Dribben, D.
5. Young, J.
6. Bell, R.
7. Fleming, R.
8. Osborn, J. R.
9. Hiltz, W.
10. Arkley, T.

# 1986 USCA SANCTIONED TOURNAMENTS

## USCA NATIONALS

National Club Team Championships
USCA National Singles and Doubles Championships

## USCA REGIONALS

Central: Bourbonnais, Illinois
Mid Atlantic: Long Island, New York
New England: Newport, Rhode Island
Southern: Hilton Head, South Carolina
Western: Seattle, Washington

## INVITATIONALS

Addison Hill Invitational
Arizona Open
Beach Club Invitational
Bermuda Invitational
Blantyre Invitational
Delaware Invitational
Gasparilla Invitational
Greenbrier Invitational
Green Gables Invitational

Hampton Court Invitational
Madden's Invitational
New Hampshire Invitational
Palm Beach Invitational
Port Royal Invitational
Round Island Invitational
San Francisco Open
Southern Cal. Invitational
Williamette Invitational

## CLUB CHAMPIONSHIPS

Arizona Croquet Club
Beach Club
Boston Croquet Club
Hempstead Croquet Club
Newport Croquet Club
New York Croquet Club

Palm Beach Croquet Club
Perrysburg Croquet Club
Rancho Santa Fe Croquet Club
San Francisco Croquet Club
Santa Rosa Croquet Club
Quantuck Bay Croquet Group

# USCA NATIONAL CHAMPIONSHIPS
## 1986

### SINGLES

1. Reid Fleming
2. Debbie Prentis
3. John C. Osborn
4. Ray Bell
5. Barry Fitzpatrick
   Mike Lufkin
7. Jim Dushek
   John Young
9. Andrew Aiken
   Garth Eliassen
   Walt Janitz
   Tom Lufkin
13. Jim Erwin
    Mike Gibbons
    Bob Kroeger
    Hans Peterson
17. Carl Behnke
    Butch Bessette
    Lisle Guernsey
    Xandra Kayden
    Howard Kellogg
    Brooke Loening
    Jane Lufkin
    Maurice Marsac
25. Dave Dondero
    Dana Dribben
    Mike Hart
    Merlin Karlock
    Dick Mathews
    Ellery McClatchy
    Chris Overly
    Nelga Young

33. Bob Alman
    Tremaine Arkley
    Jean Arrington
    Mike Burch
    Jack Hight
    Will Hiltz
    Dave Hull
    Drew Juvinall
    Dan Lindblom
    Bert Myer
    Mike Orgill
    Jack R. Osborn
    Richard Reedy
    Ned Skinner
    C.B. Smith
    Larry Wittler
49. Lila Baitschova
    Bill Campbell
    Foxy Carter
    Norman Cook
    Gunnar Erickson
    Jacque Fitzpatrick
    Jim Franck
    Franklin Friday
    Matthew Friday
    Merrit Jacob
    Bill Langstroth
    Mickey Lawson
    Jim Miles
    Ben Smith
    Fred Supper
    Richard Tucker

# DOUBLES

1. Ray Bell & Dana Dribben
2. Tremaine Arkley & Reid Fleming
3. Jim Erwin & Will Hiltz
4. Debbie Prentis & John Young
5. Carl Behnke & Lisle Guernsey
   Dave Dondero & Mike Orgill
7. Andrew Aiken & Chris Overly
   Garth Eliassen & Jane Lufkin
9. Mike Burch & Drew Juvinall
   Gunnar Erickson & Ellery McClatchy
   Mike Lufkin & Tom Lufkin
   Jack Osborn & John Osborn
13. Barry & Jacque Fitzpatrick
    Mike Hart & Walt Janitz
    Merrit Jacob & Maurice Marsac
    Hans Peterson & C.B. Smith
17. Peyton Ballenger & Nelga Young
    Norman Cook & Jim Miles
    Jim Franck & Howard Kellogg
    Cynthia & Mike Gibbons
    Jack Hight & Fred Supper
    Merlin Karlock & Richard Reedy
    Xandra Kayden & Bob Kroeger
    Dick Mathews & Larry Wittler
25. Lila Baitschova & Mickey Lawson
    Butch Bessette & Brooke Loening
    Bill & Marjorie Campbell
    Foxy Carter & Joy Waters
    Mike & Susie Hanner
    Dave Hull & Bert Myer
    Dan Lindblom & Ned Skinner
    Ben Smith & Richard Tucker
33. Bob Alman & Jim Dushel
    Jean Arrington & Libby Newell
    Matthew Friday & Franklin Friday
    Bill Langstroth & Drew McReynolds
    Dick Marsellus & Jim Torian

# USCA NATIONAL CHAMPIONS

## SINGLES

| *Year* | *Winners* | *Runner-Up* |
|------|---------|-----------|
| 1977 | J. Archie Peck, Palm Beach | Jack R. Osborn, NY |
| 1978 | Richard Pearman, Bermuda | Jack R. Osborn, NY |
| 1979 | J. Archie Peck, Palm Beach | Richard Pearman, Bermuda |
| 1980 | J. Archie Peck, Palm Beach | Arthur Bohner, NY |
| 1981 | Richard Pearman, Bermuda | Jack R. Osborn, NY |
| 1982 | J. Archie Peck, Palm Beach | Richard Pearman, Bermuda |
| 1983 | Ted Prentis, Florida & NY | Richard Pearman, Bermuda |
| 1984 | James Bast, Phoenix | Kiley Jones, NY |
| 1985 | Ray Bell, Scottsdale | John C. Osborn, NY |
| 1986 | Reid Fleming, Puget Sound | Debbie Prentis, Palm Beach |

## DOUBLES

| *Year* | *Winners* | *Runners-Up* |
|------|---------|------------|
| 1977 | Jack Osborn & J. Archie Peck | Nelga & John Young |
| 1978 | Ted Prentis & Art Bohner | Jack Osborn & Archie Peck |
| 1979 | Jack Osborn & Archie Peck | Ted Prentis & Art Bohner |
| 1980 | Ted & Ned Prentis | Dick Pearman & John Young |
| 1981 | Ted & Ned Prentis | Dick Pearman & John Young |
| 1982 | Archie & Mark Burchfield | Jack Osborn & Archie Peck |
| 1983 | Kiley Jones & R. Illingworth | Archie Peck & Dana Dribben |
| 1984 | James Bast & Ray Bell | Dick Pearman & John Young |
| 1985 | Dana Dribben & Ray Bell | Jack & John Osborn |
| 1986 | Dana Dribben & Ray Bell | Reid Fleming & T. Arkley |

# USCA NATIONAL CLUB TEAM CHAMPIONSHIPS

| Year | Winners | Runners-Up |
|------|---------|------------|
| 1980 | New York Croquet Club<br>Jack Osborn & Ted Prentis | Westhampton Mallet Club<br>Al Heath & Ned Prentis |
| 1981 | New York Croquet Club<br>Jack Osborn & Ted Prentis | Aulander Croquet Club<br>Francis Tayloe & Mac Penwell |
| 1982 | New York Croquet Club<br>Jack Osborn & Ted Prentis | Arizona Croquet Club<br>James Bast & Stanley Patmor |
| 1983 | New York Croquet Club<br>Jack Osborn & John Osborn | Palm Beach Polo & Country Club<br>Dana Dribben & Ted Prentis |
| 1984 | Arizona Croquet Club<br>Ray Bell & Ed Cline | New York Croquet Club<br>R. Illingworth & Kiley Jones |
| 1985 | Arizona Croquet Club<br>Ren Kraft & Don Stallings | New York Croquet Club<br>Jack Osborn & John Osborn |
| 1986 | New York Croquet Club<br>Jack Osborn & John Osborn | Palm Beach Polo & Country Club<br>Dana Dribben & Ted Prentis |

## US/INTERNATIONAL CHALLENGE CUP

| 1981 | USA–1 | England–15 |
|------|-------|------------|
| 1982 | USA–8 | South Africa–10 |
|      | USA–7 | Scotland–7 |
| 1983 | USA–11 | Bermuda–5 |
|      | USA–15 | Canada–1 |
| 1984 | USA–8 | Australia–16 |
| 1985 | USA–11 | Ireland–13 |
| 1986 | USA–17 | *International<br>Champions–13 |

*Great Britain, Scotland, South Africa,
Canada, Bermuda Champions

# ROQUE CLUBS

Arvin Roque Club
745 Third Avenue
Arvin, Texas

Barrington Area Roque
Club
303 West Main
Barrington, Illinois

Clinton Roque Club
521 North Mulberry
Clinton, Illinois 61727

Dallas Roque Club
5439 Vanderbilt Avenue
Dallas, Texas

Decatur Roque Club
Fairview Park
Decatur, Illinois

Eastland Roque Club
410 North Walnut
Eastland, Texas 76448

Jefferson Roque Club
500 Jefferson Building
Houston, Texas 77001

Long Beach Roque Club
Lincoln Park
Long Beach, California

Los Angeles Roque Club
Exposition Park
Los Angeles, California

Lubbock Roque Club
MacKenzie State Park
Lubbock, Texas

Orlando Roque Club
915 Broadman Street
Orlando, Florida

Portage Path Croquet Club
425 North Portage Path
Akron, Ohio 44303

Redlands Roque Club
623 East Cypress Avenue
Redlands, California

Rock Creek Roque Club
3003 South Norton
Independence, Missouri 64052

Sunshine Roque Club
Mirror Lake Park
St. Petersburg, Florida

Two-Ball Association
c/o Bixby Park Roque Club
130 Cherry Avenue
Long Beach, California 90803

Wichita Roque Club
Linwood Park
Wichita, Kansas

All roque clubs under the aegis of:
American Roque League, Inc.
4205 Briar Creek Lane
Dallas, Texas 75214

# SUPPLIERS
# OF CROQUET EQUIPMENT

Croquet International Ltd.
500 Avenue of Champions
Palm Beach Gardens, Florida
(U.S. distributor for Jaques)

Forster Manufacturing Co., Inc.
Depot Street
Wilton, Maine

Horchow Sports Collection
P.O. Box 34257
Dallas, Texas

Lilliwhite's
Southampton, New York

John Jaques and Sons, Ltd.
361 White Horse Road
Thornton Heath, Surrey
England

John Waterer, Sons and Crisp, Ltd.
Croquet Lawn Building and Maintenance
The Floral Mile
Twyford, Reading
England RG 10

Action Sportswear Specialists, Ltd.
Edments Building, 7th Floor
38 Gawler Place
Adelaide, Australia

Bert Oldfield's Sports Store
243 Pitt Street
Sydney, Australia
(Supplier of Jaques and Oliver)

Melbourne Sports Depot
121 Elizabeth Street
Melbourne, Australia

# Bibliography

## General Works:

American Roque League, Inc.: *Roque: The Game of the Century*. Dallas, 1975.

Brown, Paul: *Croquet: Rules and Strategy for Home Play*. D. Van Nostrand & Co. New York, 1957.

Carroll, Lewis: *Alice's Adventures In Wonderland*. New American Library of World Literature, Inc. New York, 1960.

Champ, Paul: *Lawn Tennis, Golf, Croquet, Polo*. 1911.

Cotter, E.P.C.: *Tackle Croquet This Way*. Stanley Paul. London, 1960.

Croquet Association: *The Laws of Association Croquet and Golf Croquet & The Regulations For Tournaments*. London, 1972.

Croquet Association: *Handbook On Modern Croquet*. Longmans Green & Co., London, 1931.

Crowther-Smith, H.F.: *The Art of Croquet: A Practical Handbook,* H., F., & G. Witherby. London, 1932.

Donaldson, Dorothy: in *World Book Encyclopedia*. Field Enterprises Educational Corporation, Chicago, 1961.

Elvey, Rev. G.F. Handel: *Croquet (Association Croquet): A Handbook On the Strokes & Tactics of the Game*. John Jaques & Son, Ltd. Surrey, 1949.

Gommes, Alice B.: *Traditional Games of England, Scotland and Ireland,* Vol. 1. Dover Publications. New York, 1964.

Heath, James Dunbar: *Complete Croquet Player*. Routelege & Son. London, 1896.

Jacobus, Charles: *Croquet and Its Rules*. American Sports Publications. New York, 1907.

Jaques, John: *Croquet: Laws and Regulations of the Game*. A. Williams, 1865.

Kayden, Xandra: *The Basics of Croquet: What It Is About, How to Play It and Rules of the American and British Association Games*. The New England Collegiate Croquet Association. Cambridge, Massachusetts, 1986.

Lauthier, Joseph: *New Rules For the Game of Mail*. Paris, 1910.

Locock, C.D.: *Modern Croquet Tactics*. 1907.

Longman, William: *Croquet In the 60's*. London, 1921.

Marx, Harpo and Barber, Roland: *Harpo Speaks*. Freeway Press, Inc. New York, 1974.

McGowan, B.C.: *By-Laws, Rules and Regulations of the Two-Ball and Royal Roque*. American Roque League, Inc. Dallas, 1957.

Menke, Frank G.: *Encyclopedia of Sports*. A.S. Barnes & Co. New York, 1953.

Miller, David and Thorp, Rupert: *Croquet and How To Play It*. Faber and Faber. London, 1966.

Nabokov, Vladimir: *Pnin*. Avon Books. New York, 1953.

National Croquet Association, Inc.: *Croquet*. Oklahoma City, 1963.

Omerod, Dr. G.I.: *Know the Game: Croquet*. Educational Productions, Ltd. Yorkshire, 1971.

Perkes, Dan: *Official Associated Press Sports Almanac*. Dell Publishing Co. New York, 1975.

Prior, Richard Chandler Alexander: *Notes on Croquet and Some Ancient Bat and Ball Games Related To It*. London, 1872.

Reckitt, Maurice Benington: *Croquet Today*. McDonald. London, 1954.

Reckitt, Maurice Benington *et. al.:* in *Encyclopeida Brittanica*. Encyclopedia Brittanica Inc. Chicago, 1964.

Reid, Captain Mayne A.: *Croquet: A Treatise With Notes and Commentary*. Publishing Office of 119 Nassau Street. New York, 1869.

Ross, Arthur G.: *Croquet and How To Play It*. Wellington, Wedderspoon & Co. London, 1947.

Ross, Arthur G.: *Croquet Handbook*. Nicholas Kaye. London, 1959.

Routelege, Edmund: *Beaddles' Dime Handbook of Croquet*. New York, 1866.

Rover, A.: *Croquet: Its Principles and Rules*. M. Bradley & Co., Springfield, 1871. 13th Edition

Schultz, Nikki: *Backyard Games*. Grosset & Dunlap. New York, 1975.

Scudder, Horace Elisha: *The Game of Croquet: Its Appointments and Laws*. Hurd & Houghton, 1865.

Solomon, J.W.: *Croquet*. B.T. Batford. London, 1966.

Teichmann, Howard: *George S. Kaufman: An Intimate Biography*. Atheneum Books. New York, 1972.

Tollemache, Bentley Lyonel John: *Croquet By Lord Tollemache*. S. Paul. London, 1914.

Wells, H.G.: *The Croquet Player: A Story*. N.C.W. Viking. New York, 1937.

Whipple, G.M. and Smith, A.A.: *Croquet: Rules and Regulations*. Salem, 1871.

Williams, L.B.: *Croquet*. A.D. Innes & Co. London, 1899.

[Anonymous]: *Croquet As Played By the Newport Croquet Club*. Sheldon & Co. New York, 1867.

## Periodicals:

Bryan, Robert: 'Croquet Is Not a Silly Game.' *M Magazine,* July 1984.

Gammon, Clive: 'A Wicket Championship.' *Sports Illustrated,* May 27, 1987.

Hart, Moss: 'East-West Croquet.' *Life,* July 22, 1946.

Jenks, Tudor: 'Antiquarian Athletics.' *Outing,* January 1909.

Johnston, Lonn: 'Croquet—A New Breed of Competitors.' *Los Angeles Times,* September 30, 1986.

Keteyian, Armen: 'Footloose.' *Sports Illustrated,* April 1983.

Kinsman, Dorothy: 'Navy Takes Croquet Cup.' *The St. John's Reporter,* June 1987.

Kleinfeld, N.R.: 'Executive Fun and Games.' *The New York Times Sunday Magazine, Part 2,* June 8, 1986.

Kornbluth, Jesse: 'With Mallets Aforethought, Croquet Comes Back.' *The New York Times Sunday Magazine,* September 14, 1980.

Maas, Peter: 'Sport of Stings.' *Holiday,* October 1967.

MacKenzie, Sir Compton: 'Croquet: The Ideal Pastime.' *Spectator,* July 2, 1954.

Mallalieu, J.P.W.: 'Perfection on the Lawn.' *Spectator,* July 17, 1953.

Mathus, K.: 'Croquet Tips.' *Popular Science,* August 1945.

Mathewson, Joseph: 'Right Out of Their League.' *Sports Illustrated,* April 5, 1971.

Olezewska, E.S. and Ross, Alan S.C.: 'Hong Kong in Croquet.' *Notes and Queries,* September 1965.

Parker, Suzy: 'Join a Club: Take a Whack at Croquet.' *USA Today,* July 8, 1986.

Ross, Alan S.C.: 'Croquet.' *Notes and Queries,* September 1968.

White, Timothy: 'Steve Winwood's Merging Traffic.' *Musician Magazine,* July 1986.

*Australian Croquet Council Gazette,* April, 1975.

'Awfully Good Show.' *Time,* July 31, 1950.

'Croquet.' *Canada,* June 1921.

'Croquet At Eighty-Two: With Rules Adopted At Louisville, Kentucky.' *Recreation,* March 1936.

'Croquet: Favorite Form of Recreation.' *Recreation,* July 1948.

'Croquet Golf.' *Playground,* November 1929.

'Croquet Golf Courses on Playgrounds.' *Recreation,* March 1931.

'Croquet Is For Everyone.' *Popular Gardener,* March 1966.

'Croquet Lives.' *Newsweek,* July 30, 1973.

'Croquet: Social Shock Absorber.' *Arts and Decoration,* August 1932.

'Cue Roque Table.' *Industrial Arts,* January 1929.

'Figure Croquet Wickets Of Sheet Metal Are Quite Easily Seen.' *Popular Mechanics,* May 1941.

'In the Days Of Croquet.' *Freeman,* May 30, 1923.

'Lawn Bowlers' Controversy.' New York *Times,* May 4, 1972.

'Mallets Across the Blinkin' Sea.' *Sports Illustrated,* July 31, 1967.

'Mallet Men Of Manhattan.' *Christian Science,* October 1937.

'New Croquet Roque.' *Collier's,* August 12, 1911.

'Outdoor Recreation At Night.' *Suburban Life,* August 1907.

'Roque As A Suburban Pastime.' *Suburban Life,* March 1911.

'Roque: Modern Croquet.' *Outing,* September 1901.

'Sticky Wicket.' *Newsweek,* August 29, 1966.

*United States Croquet Association Croquet Gazette,* 1987 Edition.